# POLYMER
## The Chameleon Clay

Victoria Hughes

P9-CKE-111

© 2002 by Victoria Hughes

All rights reserved.

No portion of this publication may be reproduced or transmitted in any form or by any means, electronic or mechanical, including photocopy, recording, or any information storage and retrieval system, without permission in writing from the publisher, except by a reviewer who may quote brief passages in a critical article or review to be printed in a magazine or newspaper, or electronically transmitted on radio or television.

Published by

**krause publications**

700 East State Street • Iola, WI 54990-0001
715/445-2214 • FAX: 715/445-4087   www.krause.com

Krause Publications
700 E. State St.
Iola, WI 54990-0001
Telephone 715-445-2214
www.krause.com

Please call or write for our free catalog of publications. Our toll-free number to place an order or obtain a free catalog is 800-258-0929 or please use our regular business telephone, 715-445-2214.

Library of Congress Catalog Number: 2002107601

ISBN: 0-87349-373-7

Printed in the United States of America

Illustrations by Victoria Hughes
Photos by Victoria Hughes unless otherwise indicated

The following product or company names appear in this book: Atlas Pasta Machines, Bakelite™, Beadalon™, Cernit™, Dragon Skin™, Dremel™, Eberhard Faber, Fimo™, Fimo™ Art Translucent, Fimo™ Classic, Fimo™ Gloss Varnish, Fimo™ Pulver, Fimo™ Soft, Fimo™ Translucent, Fordham, Frisbee™, Golden™, Golden Artists Colors™, Golden™ Polymer Varnish, Jacquard™ Pearl-Ex, Liquid Sculpey, Liquitex™, Mix-Quick, Mylar™, Polyform™, Prēmo, Prēmo Translucent With Bleach, PVC, Saran Wrap™, Sculpey™, Sculpey™ Flex, Slo-Zap™, Sobo, Softflex, Speedball™, Super Glue, Translucent Liquid Sculpey, Treasure Gold™, Trizact™, X-acto™, Zap-a-Gap™

THE THINGS THAT MAKE US HAPPY MAKE US
WISE ~John Crowley,
"LITTLE BIG"
♡

Victoria Hughes, *Safe
Travel Passes*, 1997.

And for Joyous Jeanne! With lots of
for
romping fiery
enthusiasm for
Margaret and James Hughes,
your creative
Jeremy Jacobs Gordon,
EXPANSION
Martin Ambrose Mayer,
and Robert K. Liu.

Thank you for sharing
the story of Jeanne in    thank you    Tony Hughes
my studio!                            Santa Fe, July 2012

# table of contents

## Chapter 5: Introductory Projects 72

## Chapter 6: Intermediate Projects 111

## Gallery 132

## About the Author 138

## Templates 139

## Resources 143

# an introduction to the imitative techniques

Victoria Hughes, *Inlaid Box*, 2002.
A myriad of imitative techniques,
colors, textures, translucencies, and
opacities are shown on this
hexagonal box lid.

Re-creating a material requires first and foremost that you really notice the material. Absorb the texture of the sandstone, the depth of color in the jade, the incredible complexity of lace agate, the versatility and responsiveness of polymer clay, the creative curiosity of your own mind. Learn, by observing the world around you, to love this planet and its attributes, by fully entering your life's experience. The first page of my class handouts says only, "You must be present to win."

Imitative techniques with polymer clay incorporate sophisticated clay body mixing, painting, carving, sanding, polishing, voluptuous attention to surfaces, and an evocation of other times and perhaps other cultures. The techniques encourage you to master polymer clay and to master your own perceptual processes as well.

I developed these techniques through my fascination with polymer clay, inspired by the natural world and by the work of Gwen Gibson, a talented artist from the Bay Area. I needed a source for the antique and exotic elements I was using in my jewelry, and realized I would have the widest selection (at the best prices) if I made them myself. Gwen was interested in creating a variety of gorgeous surface effects involving painting and working back through the paint. I was always interested in the clay body itself, and polymer's unique ability to be both color and volume at the same time. Combining these two interests led me to the imitative techniques, which use polymer's promiscuity with other materials to combine and create any color, translucency, and texture of clay body imaginable, and continue with paints, patinas, and surface actions like carving or polishing, to generate beautifully seductive materials.

I have two goals when teaching these techniques: First, that you learn to observe the physical world more clearly and decide if things are as you want them, realizing your ability to make them how you think they should be; Second, that you understand polymer clay more thoroughly and increase your proficiency and skills with this versatile material. *See* what you're looking at and respond with knowledge and skill.

These techniques were not developed to fool people into believing that the polymer is the authentic material. After all the work involved, why deny you made it yourself?

I developed and teach these approaches at my teaching center, the ArtRanch, to expand your creative options and inspire new technical and conceptual directions. The ArtRanch is a place for creative action of all types. I host a variety of artists, performers, and teachers. It is not only about polymer clay and mixed media, but about creative expression in general.

The ArtRanch has both a physical location (presently in New Mexico) and a virtual location (wherever you and I are in class together). When you are working with this book, you are at the ArtRanch, just as you are when you are watching my instructional videos or in a class with me in New York or Seattle.

As you read through this book, you'll notice a few underlying concepts. These are basic concepts for creative action. Consider for a moment that all of life is creative action. Art is just the tip of the iceberg.

## there are no mistakes

Do it and see what happens. Anything you didn't expect is new information, not an error. Based on new information, decide how you want to do it next time. Everything has a purpose: that thing that looks like a mistake is no exception. What do you see?

## remember who you are

You are a unique human being, with a purposeful blend of characteristics. Don't try to be someone else, or make their work. Be you. You are the only one who can be you, the best you there is. You are here to learn and be and do what is true for you, not anyone else.

## of course you can

Of course you can do whatever it is. You have much more wisdom, perception, and strength than you normally reveal. Investigate your self and you'll realize this is true. See those beautiful mountains; don't let doubt show you a hill. Rely on the real you, now.

## do it now, no more waiting

Stop waiting. Do it now, even if it's a little thing you could put off until later. Learn from this how good it feels to finally take action, and patiently take back your momentum. The journey of a thousand miles begins with one step, and you can do that now.

Life, like art, is an ongoing process. There are no wrong answers.

# before you begin

# a word about
# making things

$t$veryone likes to make things. Some people feel more satisfied with their results than others, but everyone enjoys the process. Let's look at how you make things, and what you can do to develop an easy, personalized response to whatever project you embark upon.

Five basic principles help channel all that energy you have into a completed project that satisfies you personally. After years of listening to and teaching adults, I offer these principles to help you focus your energy and succeed in whatever creative projects you set for yourself. Try them.

1. **start with what works**
2. **know your intention**
3. **allow experiments**
4. **take care of your tools**
5. **act on your intuition**

## start with what works

The first principle establishes your foundation. First, identify your own creative successes and observe what circumstances surrounded those moments. What works physically for you? Remember your most fulfilling creative experience. Allow the memory of that situation to surround you now. Recall it with all your senses. Where are you? Are there people around? Is there music? What kind? Is it day or night? What are you wearing? What experiences led to the mood you are in? What colors, smells, and kind of air are around you? Take a moment now and identify everything you can remember about what works for you.

Now ask the same questions, this time about what works emotionally and conceptually. What excites you, you wonderful unique human? What pleases you, gets you grinning? What do you really love? If you could experience anything, what is that thing? What are your delights and passions?

Victoria Hughes, *Feathered Pot*, 2000. First make things for your own enjoyment and education. While I was developing the body, and therefore personality, of this happy vessel, the character seemed to ask for the colors and textures of this lovely collection of feathers. He balances on his tail.

What are your deep simple truths? What works metaphysically for you? Make a poem of these things, or a song, or a list on your favorite paper.

Let go of others' definitions and assumptions about what an artist's life looks like. Everyone's creative process is different. Yours is exquisitely tuned to support the creative gifts you have been given. Give yourself the things that work for you, and you're already on the path of greater creative response. You have begun to reintegrate yourself into your life and actions.

## know your intention

The second principle addresses a basic question. Why are you making something now? What do you hope to accomplish with this creative gesture? When you know your intention, it's easy to calmly select and use materials that will accomplish your intention. However if it's not identified, the lack of a clear purpose or intention can knot your creative flow into a tight little self-referential ball. It can feel paralyzing. Many of the blocks I see in my students stem from a lack of clear intention.

For instance, your intention right now may be to "experiment with new materials," "make a present for my sister," "make retail items in the $50 range," or "create sculpture illustrating my spiritual beliefs." It may be "goofing around to see what happens, which might also relieve this tension headache." All intentions are valid. Choose one for this moment and follow it with conviction and vitality.

Imagine you are sitting down right now to make something. What's the job of the object you're making? I am not asking you what the object is, I am asking why you want to make something. If you

don't know why you are making something, how will you ever feel satisfied by what you made? There are no wrong answers here, nothing to judge, just a choice to make. Make it, do it, and then you can draw on more information for your next choice.

If you are at a crossroads and don't choose the direction you want to go, you can spend your energy until eternity circling the crossroads, never getting anywhere. When you select an intention, your choice of materials, inspirations, and actions for this goal will be obvious.

## allow experiments

By definition, the creative process opens up possibilities. When something unexpected happens, or a tempting detour keeps whispering to you, don't judge it as a mistake. Instead look closely at it, listen to its message, and see how you can incorporate it into your work. If something suggests itself to you while you are in midstream, try it. Then decide how or whether to use it.

Think back to the crossroads of intention. If you decide early on that you already know the only and best route to your destination, you are going to be frustrated when detours show up. You might not take advantage of an unexpected town that appears, full of interesting people and unusual opportunities. Go ahead, explore this new situation to see what it offers that is congruent to your intention. In my experience, there are no accidents, just as there are no mistakes. It's like those rope and pipe jungle gyms on playgrounds: there are hundreds of fun ways to climb all over them, but first you have to decide to climb at all.

Court the unexpected, follow up on that mischievous, impish concept, that new technical idea that's teasing you. Try it now, observe how it supports your intention. Your intention will remain firm here, you are always in charge. Experiments allow the universe to add its support to your intention. It makes sense to accept the help.

## take care of your tools

Body, mind, and spirit. Although we tend to think of our toolbox as holding pliers, blades, X-acto knives, etc., those are just "little tools"—extensions that our "big tools" use for detail work. The big tools need maintenance even more. Little tools can be replaced. The big tools—your body, mind, and spirit—are the structure of that channel mentioned earlier, through which creative energy moves.

Blocks and fears can temporarily obstruct that channel, but you are designed for free-flowing energy. Whenever things don't feel easy and active, there are adjustments to be done: never confuse the block with who you are.

Making things involves all of you, your whole self. A successful, fulfilling creative life will flourish if your whole self is flourishing. That's why it's so much fun. Sometimes when it's hard to make things, it's because a big tool needs attention. If your art-making feels blocked, check in with yourself. What really makes you feel happy and well? Have you been getting enough fresh air? Taken the opportunity to move briskly, doing something you love, like dancing or Frisbee playing? Had some time with yourself? Are you sleeping well? Move more, watch a little less TV. Keep your own channel coming in with the best reception.

Easy and satisfying art-making comes from a balanced mental, physical, emotional, and spiritual system. Keep your big tools in good working condition. That old outdated model of unhealthy, unhappy artists struggling to survive is not useful or accurate. Of course they struggled. They felt terrible. They were trying to drive to California with flat tires and a bad alternator. You don't need to do that. Strong, personally satisfying creativity flows easily through a healthy system.

## act on your intuition

Listen to your intuition, trust it, and act on it. Creativity is a web that extends throughout your conscious and unconscious awareness. To access all of that web, to be as creative as you'd like in any moment, draw on your noncognitive awareness as well. The way you download from this web is through listening to your intuition. Intuition is your whole self talking to you from a holographic knowledge. Respect it and use the information you give yourself. In fact, your intuition is a very big tool. Trusting intuition maintains it and increases your ability to listen and act on it more. Acting on it when it presents itself maintains it. Do it now, no waiting.

What do you think you're really doing when you make something? All aspects of your self come together in these magnificent moments when you move stuff around, do a little of this, a little of that, and voila! You create something that has not existed anywhere in the universe until you (you!) just made it. You took the pure energy of your idea and gave it a physical form. The communication that flows through you, linking that idea and the physical form, is creativity. Contemplate it. Creativity is a spiritual act.

# a word about color

Color is fundamental to your sensory experience. Our relationship to color is so profound that I have gone into it at more length in the next section (see page 50). Revel in colors, enjoy them like a gourmand finding the first fresh fig of the summer. Be as voluptuous and indulgent as possible with color. Observe the colors around you. In working with polymer, always mix your own colors and persevere until you have exactly what you want.

Color enfolds you in a sensuous, physical presence. In fact, when I am developing a new technique or teasing out a complex concept, I deliberately reduce my palette of colors because a full spectrum can seduce me away from the delicacy of my seedling idea.

Your contract as an artist is to select or create the materials that work for you specifically. Always mix your own colors of polymer clay. The 40 or so generic clay colors that come in those crisp little packages are just a tiny fraction of the colors you actually see around you.

The human eye can distinguish two million different colors. This gives you a sense of color as unique and distinctive as a fingerprint. Nature uses all of those two million visible colors in its work and then lopes off into territories of color you can't see: ultraviolets, infrareds, frequencies of the electromagnetic spectrum we don't even know about yet. "Color" is nothing more than a section of the electromagnetic vibrational river that your optic nerves perceive and can relay to your brain to be interpreted visually. But color's true identity is pure vibration.

Your biological system swims in this ocean of vibration: it feels real and natural to you. Humans evolved into it. Remember being a kid, wanting the biggest box of crayons? Even with 120 crayons, you had the feeling there were more colors you weren't getting. You were right.

You respond to the vibration of color by reflex first. Like sea anemones in tidal pools, instinctively pulling in their tendrils in response to changes in the waves washing over them, you viscerally experience color, intuitively moving toward or away, wanting more or less, being curious, stimulated, or soothed by colors. This can frequently happen below your conscious awareness.

This pre-verbal response may be followed by an analytical response. You may use your mind

Victoria Hughes, *Souvenir 3 – Oh Clever Butterfly,* 1999. This sculptural box, with a drawer that opens to a cascading poem, is about delight and transformation. Color is a fundamental expressive tool. The imitative techniques bring together color, texture, and also integrate cultures, histories, and preciousness. The carved and gilded Sanskrit at the top reads "namaste," or "I greet the Divine within you."

to understand and interpret your visceral experience. Thus color theory and mathematical analyses of color are useful art-making techniques. They help you analyze and duplicate colors, giving you further control over your art. You can become a master of color by allowing these two responses—the instinctive and the analytical—to work together. Color is visual jazz: intuition, and knowledge at once.

Many resources exist for analyzing color. There are wonderful books that teach the use of the color wheel. If you are not familiar with the basics of color-mixing, get one of these books and teach yourself. Please consider these books as appendices to your own internal book of color. Collect the data you require from these books to support your experience but don't look to these books to tell you your experience. Direct experience of your life is the only thing that will allow you to understand and master it.

The more variety of color that's in your pieces, even as subtle variations of related hues, the more realistic your pieces will look. This is especially true for pieces that mimic natural materials. You'll notice, for example, that there is very little pure black or pure white in nature but there are innumerable variations of near-blacks and off-whites. One small chip of jasper can have more different browns, blacks, and whites than you could mix in a week.

To master the imitative techniques, observe the colors that appear in the objects you want to re-create, then mix those colors of polymer. For instance, look at antique ivory and check for yourself what combination of clays will re-create the colors you see, rather than using my recipe for ivory as if it were the only true formula.

Polymer clay has an added, unique edge over other art media because the material always has a color. In polymer, color and form must be mutually considered from the beginning. Evaluation of a polymer clay form is always linked to response to its color. Other materials are either colors or forms and these aspects must be considered separately, then combined later. Polymer allows you to simultaneously create a three-dimensional form and control its color.

Colors are always perceived in relationships. Whenever your eyes are open, your visual field is picking up millions of small areas of color. Unless you are holding a color swatch right against your eyeball, any color you see is being perceived as an element that is interacting with other colors. Even with the color swatch, light reflecting across the paper causes subtle changes throughout its color.

Be aware of this when working. For example, notice how you respond to vermilion red when it is a thin, calligraphic line floating in a vast field of bright blue. Compare that to your response to a square field of vermilion red covered with tiny black squares. The same color, different visceral experiences. Experiment with this effect in your work. See how you respond, and what creates the color sensation you want.

Keep a color journal or logbook full of magazine pages, scraps of fabrics, photographs—anything you respond to is valid information. Use this personal color library to inspire new mixes in polymer clay bodies and to expand your habitual color palette. Add notes on color relationships.

After working with thousands of students, I can confidently say that everyone has a personal sense of what works for them. Try this yourself and trust your own responses. It's as easy as that.

# a word about variation

*N*ature is a model for variation. Nature tries everything. It is supportive and nurturing to all kinds of life. This is an artist's attitude. You may have noticed this already, looking around the planet. "Why make one kind of bug when I can make six million?" is nature's basic approach. "Why just make birds that go in the air? Why not birds that go underwater, and birds that live in caves, and birds that sing, and birds who don't fly at all but run really fast, and mammals and fish that look like birds?"

Variation rules, no question. The criterion is "and," not "or." This is the approach to have with your own creative process. Don't fear the experiment, the random occurrence, the unpredictable gesture. Try everything so you know what you like and how to get it.

Look at it another way. There aren't many ideas that haven't existed somewhere in the natural world. One example that particularly touches me is a species of small spider that lives exclusively in the snowfields of the Himalayan Mountains. High up on the ice, these delicate creatures spend their lives in the cold air and bright light. They survive because of the huge air masses that roll up the Indian subcontinent and run into the wall of the Himalayas. These thick air masses are rich with particles of organic materials, pollen, and dirt picked up as the air moves over thousands of miles of earth, farm, and forest. The sole food of these spiders is broken-up bits of bugs, carried in this cloud of fine detritus and blown into the crevasses in the snow and ice.

The variations in the natural world astonish and mesmerize. We evolved our human sense of aesthetics surrounded by the wanton, delicious, endless experimentation of nature. Variation is what reads as *right* to us. Right is not one object perfectly duplicated, it is an infinite number of related objects, all slightly different. Obviously nature does not have a problem with experimenting. Why should you?

When it comes to your art, there is no one way to make something. Even in the imitative techniques, the goal is to re-create or interpret a possible version of the material, not to duplicate a specific object from that material. Learn the techniques, follow the directions so you understand which actions create which results. Once you know how to get what you want, play, experiment, follow your intuition. Any little urge you have to say "What if?" demands to be acted on as part of your creative contract. So encourage variation. Mix an unusual color. Make odd marks, try a different tool, use a new kind of paint. Follow your sense of curiosity. And if you ever feel you should hold back, just remember that there are six million kinds of bugs.

Victoria Hughes, *Ivory Neckpiece,* 1999. Multiple layers of indigo transfer, staining, and carving on an imitative ivory polymer just seemed to go with the basic image, a Japanese woodcut from the 1600s. The design carries around to the back of the piece.

chapter 2

# imitative
# techniques with
# polymer clay

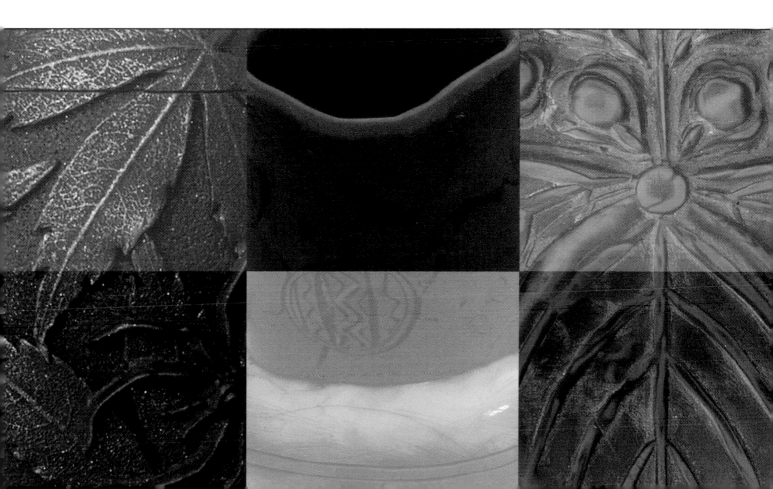

Imitative techniques develop two things—your skilled perception of the world you inhabit, and your mastery of polymer clay. Once you learn these concepts, you will be able to generate almost any effect you can imagine in polymer clay and mixed media.

The first of these goals—skilled perception—accomplishes itself in simple daily activities, done with attention. What specific color is your favorite shirt? How translucent is a sheet of paper with morning sunlight shining through it? What other textures are like those of your favorite shoes? How smooth or rough is the surface you are sitting on at this moment? What shapes do you most enjoy holding or exploring with your fingers? Think of a small special object you treasure. Where does it come from? Does looking at it bring you more fully into the present, or take you somewhere else? What culture does it evoke?

The second of these goals—mastering polymer clay—will be unavoidably met as you investigate, learn, and practice the techniques. Imitative techniques embrace many different approaches to polymer clay. Making such things as ancient ivory, jade, or honeyed amber is so satisfying that taking in the technical knowledge to do it is effortless. Polymer clay's versatility means you can create any color, then make it almost any translucency, add pretty much anything into the clay body to change its texture, work the clay with techniques applicable to a soft malleable material (before baking), or to a solid, hard material (after baking), and on and on.

To accurately mimic a material using polymer clay, closely observe its visual and tactile qualities. Use categories that correspond to polymer clay characteristics. These four categories are *color, translucency/opacity, surface,* and *patina.* By identifying these four qualities and re-creating each in turn, you will conjure the material that combines those qualities. It's a synergy of effects.

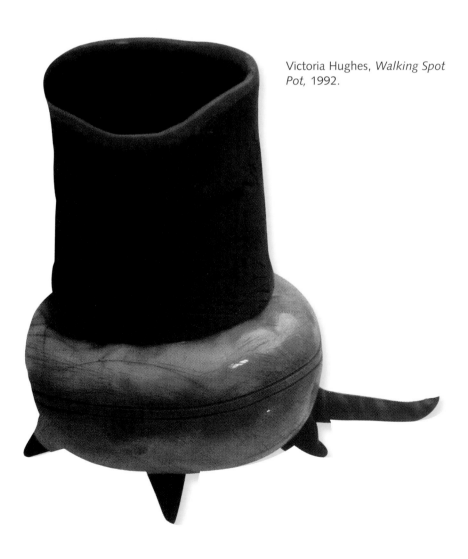

Victoria Hughes, *Walking Spot Pot,* 1992.

FINISH ALL STEPS *before* JUDGING!

Imitative techniques work in tandem. Until you have done all of them to your piece, you won't know what your work will look like. Respect your work; finish it, then judge it.

The basic concept is *finish all steps before judging.* Only when you have re-created all those qualities can you judge their effectiveness. These qualities are cumulative. Until you have finished buffing your piece, you won't know how successful your work is. Take it from someone who knows.

## note

*The imitative techniques are a specialized branch of polymer clay. Many reference books are available for more general polymer information. Several are listed on pages 143-144.*

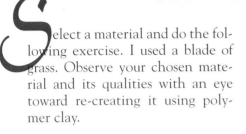

# a perceptual exercise

Select a material and do the following exercise. I used a blade of grass. Observe your chosen material and its qualities with an eye toward re-creating it using polymer clay.

### color

Natural materials are rarely a single color. Even grass is a combination of greens. When observing the color of the material you want to mimic, assess the warmth or coolness of the color. Does the predominate color tend toward the blues or toward the oranges? Check the paleness or darkness of the specific color. Is it a dull or a deep color? Vibrant or chalky? What does the color evoke? Notice how it appears in relationship to the colors around it. Does it stand out, or merge into a community of like colors?

Next, how do you mix this color? What colors of clay do you start with? What do you add to them to get exactly what you see? You will read some instruction in color mixing later in the book, but never restrict yourself to just those suggestions.

### translucency/opacity

Most organically created materials like ivory, coral, and amber have some luminosity to them. Life on this blue-green planet depends on water everywhere, including the tissues of living things. This shows up as a mild translucency. Look at the sun shining through a single blade of grass. The glowing spring green arises from light passing through water in the cells of the leaf. Contrast this luminosity to sandstone or granite, whose colors are flat. No light at all can shine through these strongly opaque materials. Calcite and other clear materials are more transparent than polymer can mimic: this is polymer's one major inadequacy. Translucent yes, transparent no. Assess the translucency of your material. Is it translucent or partially translucent? How much sense of depth does it have? Is the surface completely opaque, without luminosity?

How do you develop this luminous quality in a clay body? What ratio of opaque and translucent clays are needed to re-create it? Is the translucency grainy and pebbly, or like wax, clear of any texture? You will develop the answers to these questions by making the projects in this book and by doing further experimentation on your own.

Prēmo and Fimo make the best translucent clays for imitative techniques. Fimo's translucent clay has tiny crystalline-looking pebbles, or plaquing, that show up after baking. Prēmo makes a translucent clay that does not pebble. In all brands, the white clay is most opaque. A little white can be added to darker colors to make them more opaque without lightening the color perceptibly.

Victoria Hughes, *Jade Vessel,* 1993. I made and shaded five different translucent greens across each other to re-create the luminous jade of this vase. Baking the elements separately and adding them on in three separate steps gave me control in constructing the final form.

Nan Roche, *Pendant,* 2002. A dusty blue-green paint sparsely applied points up the subtle red and black layering of this beautiful lacquer effect.

Photo by the artist.

Photo by Don Haab.

Jacqueline Lee, *Maple Leaf Inro*, 2001. Keen attention to contrasting surface textures and a monochromatic palette of colors draw the eye along the leaves molded from real Japanese maples. The underlying rough ground unites the matte leaves and the glimmering spider.

## surface

Surface defines the physical texture and characteristics of the finish of the material. Establishing a surface may be done before and/or after baking. My blade of grass is smooth and has fine ridges parallel to the blade and a thick central vein. Is the surface of your material slick, bumpy, grainy, grooved, pitted, or matte? Surface also describes any applied details or molded relief. Is your material carved? Molded? Perfectly flat and machined? Are there any indicators of aging, like irregular pitting or cracks? Or does your material look new, shiny, precisely textured?

How can you re-create the surface quality of your material? Should you use a tool or material to emboss texture or details? Can the surface texture be applied before baking? Is it a textured translucent material? Can something be mixed into the clay to give it the texture? Does the clay need to be rigid for you to develop the texture? You will find the answer to all these questions through experimentation and by doing the projects in this book.

## patina

Patina defines the final surface treatment, rather than the surface shaping. Patina is a two-dimensional effect on top of the three-dimensional surface. Developing a patina is done after baking. In terms of these techniques, patina is the sheen on the surface, the gloss on the ivory, the verdigris blue-green on copper, the dust of the ages sifted between the carved details of an old lacquer box.

A patina is applied after all other qualities have been addressed. Patinas may be paints, dusts, waxes, sanding, polishing, or other applications. Some materials have more obvious patinas than others. Sometimes an imitative technique does not require a patina. On my blade of grass there is a faint opalescent trail along one edge (where a snail glimmered across it?). There's also a tiny trough of dust in the indentation up the center vein. What is the patina on your material? Is it slick? Layered? Worn through? Polished? Patinas reflect the age and wear on things—whether corners are rubbed off, surface textures worn down, or colors muted from years of handling.

Does the surface look fine-grained and shiny, a patina that would result from a lot of sanding and polishing? Is it matte and pitted? Are there layers of paint that have been worn away? Are the layered colors glossy or matte? What color is the dust in the hollows? Are there processes you are familiar with that might create this same effect? Consider these questions and connect them to what you have learned in other media. I provide many solutions for different patinas, surfaces, colors, and opacities in the text of this book. These solutions will serve you best when you integrate them with your own experience.

Gwen Gibson, *Wall Piece*, 1996. A riotous and effective combination of different patinas and surface treatments, applied after baking. Ranging from very rough and corroded to very shiny and worn, all patinas enhance a sense of great age.

Photo courtesy of the artist.

# materials and tools

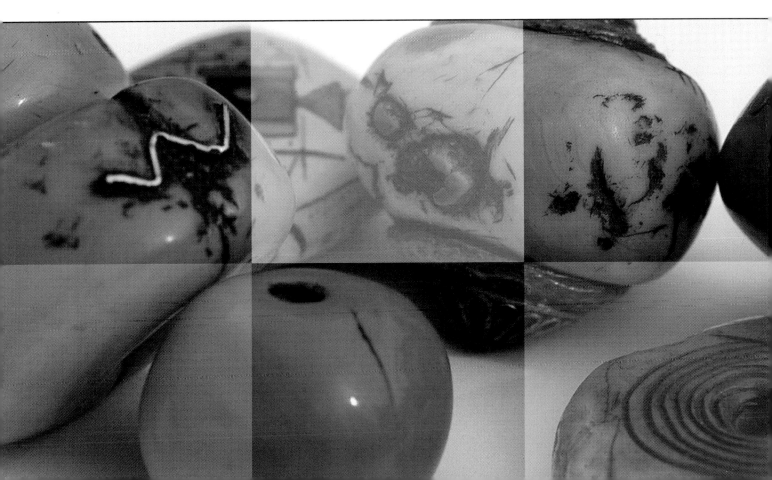

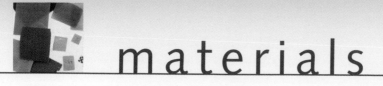

# materials

An array of polymer clays used in imitative techniques. Fimo, Prēmo, and Cernit are all malleable modeling materials; Translucent Liquid Sculpey has a distinctive honey-like consistency. The thin prebaked polymer pieces will be inlaid into unbaked clay and baked a second time.

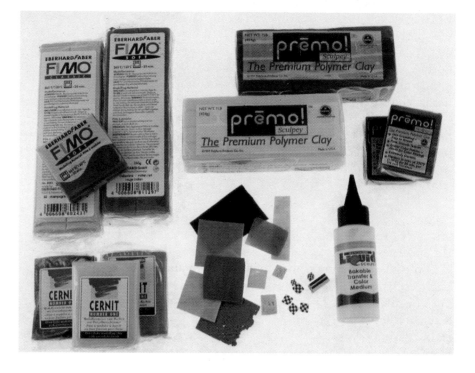

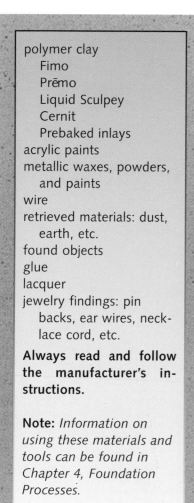

polymer clay
   Fimo
   Prēmo
   Liquid Sculpey
   Cernit
   Prebaked inlays
acrylic paints
metallic waxes, powders, and paints
wire
retrieved materials: dust, earth, etc.
found objects
glue
lacquer
jewelry findings: pin backs, ear wires, necklace cord, etc.

**Always read and follow the manufacturer's instructions.**

**Note:** *Information on using these materials and tools can be found in Chapter 4, Foundation Processes.*

**Additional note:** *A list of suppliers and resources can be found on pages 143-144.*

## polymer clay

Polymer clay is a synthetic modeling material, primarily PVC, or polyvinyl chloride, which is a type of plastic similar to the white pipes that the water in your house runs through. Polymer clay also includes opacifiers, pigments, and a plasticizer, which is a chemical that keeps the clay flexible until heated. Polymer clays are not water-based nor are they related to traditional ceramic clays in any way.

Polymer clay is very temperature-sensitive before and after hardening. The clay begins to harden when heated above 120°F; it polymerizes as the molecules connect in long chains, creating a stable structure. Once this process begins, it is no longer possible to re-model the clay.

Therefore, never leave unbaked polymer near a heat source or in direct sunlight for any length of time. Do not leave it in the car on a hot day. You get the idea.

Proper hardening, or baking, occurs when the clay remains at 275°F for at least 20 minutes. Some brands of polymer clay can be baked for an extremely long time with no ill effects. Never bake it too hot. Baking time can range widely, but temperature *must* be consistent. (Baking is discussed in more depth in Chapter 4.) Polymer clay becomes increasingly durable with a longer baking time.

The plasticizer is an oily chemical solvent whose only purpose is to soften all plastics it comes in contact with. Avoid putting unbaked clay on plastic surfaces, furniture, photocopies, books, and other absorbent or synthetic surfaces. Never let unbaked clay rest on baked clay. Any film or residue of the plasticizer on baked polymer will eventually soften and deteriorate the baked clay, no matter how well polymerized it is.

Keep your hands clean when you are working, and do your work in as clean an area as possible. Polymer clay attracts dust, dirt, animal hairs, and other airborne detritus. Always wash your hands after using this or any art material, or before you eat.

Occasionally, different polymer manufacturers reformulate their products. Changes occur primarily in color, color names, and the softness of the clay before baking. The information in this book is accurate at the time of writing, and gives you a solid overview of the qualities of the various brands.

If you have an opinion about any changes, write, e-mail, or fax both your distributor and the manufacturer, and let them know how you, as the buying public, feel about the changes. More than most, the polymer clay industry forms a very interactive community, including artists, teachers, hobbyists, and manufacturers. Manufacturers want and need to hear from you, as the end users of their products.

In the United States four brands of polymer clay are currently available, and each has slightly different qualities. These brands are Fimo, Prēmo, Cernit, and Sculpey. Fimo is manufactured in Germany by a venerable art materials company, Eberhard Faber, and was the first polymer clay marketed globally. Fimo is available in Fimo Classic, Fimo Soft, and Fimo Translucent Colors. The Prēmo and the Sculpey families of clays are both produced by Polyform Products in Illinois, who also manufacture Sculpey Flex and Liquid Sculpey. For the purposes of this book, you will use Fimo, Cernit, Prēmo, and Translucent Liquid Sculpey (TLS). You will not use the rest of the

Sculpey family or Sculpey Flex for the imitative techniques, so I will not discuss them further. Cernit is also from Europe, and is a little more difficult to find, but worth knowing about, as you'll see below. Other brands exist, but are unusual to find in this country.

Each brand exhibits its own unique range of the following characteristics: color, translucency or opacity of the clay body, textural and visual effects, softness or stiffness before baking, durability after baking, ability to tolerate multiple bakings, and ability to fuse to itself. You will notice these characteristics in your clay immediately.

All brands of clay can be mixed together. The resulting hybrid clay body is a straightforward combination of the qualities of the different brands mixed together. Thus, as you develop mastery of polymer clay, you will create custom clay bodies that have precisely the qualities you choose.

For some imitative techniques, a specific brand of clay is required. All of that technique, then, should use the same brand or a mixture of that brand of clay and another, allowing the primary clay to predominate. Otherwise your pieces will tend to delaminate as one layer peels away from a layer of a different brand.

Versatility, color, durability, and ease of use are combined in polymer clay in an art material without limits. You can create any color and texture imaginable by combining different clays from the wide range of colors and effects available, and by mixing other media into the clay body itself.

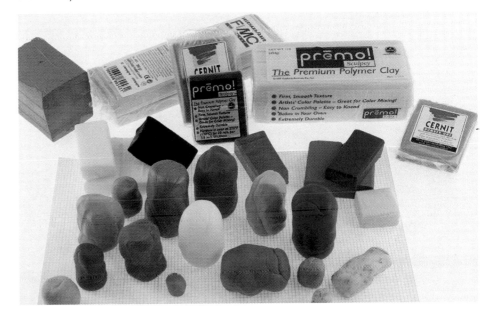

# Polymer Qualities

NOTE - THESE ARE GENERAL TENDENCIES - BATCHES MAY VARY

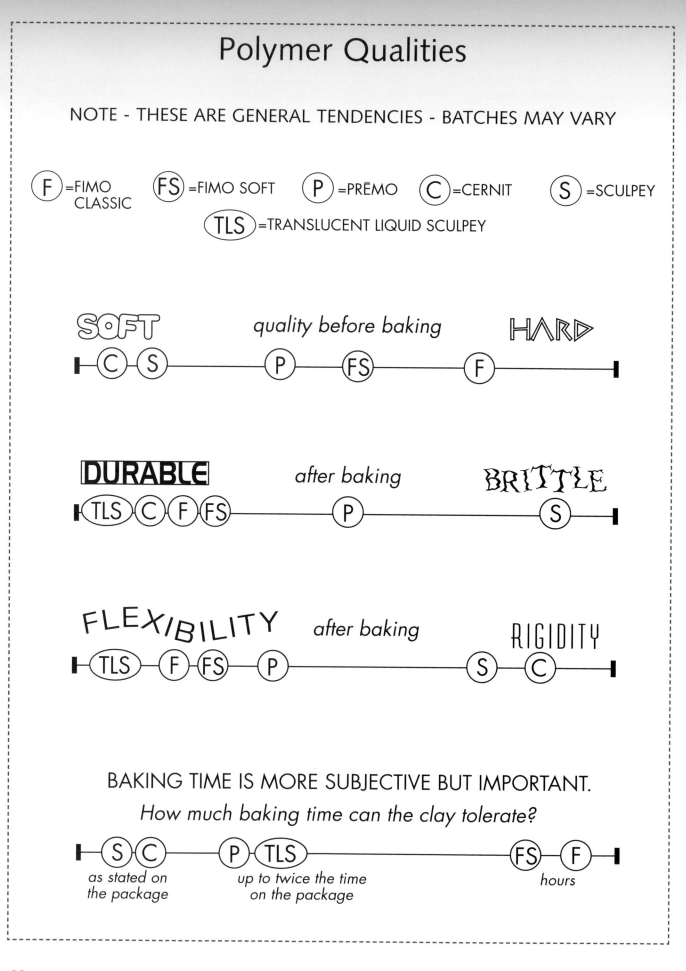

(F) =FIMO CLASSIC    (FS) =FIMO SOFT    (P) =PRĒMO    (C) =CERNIT    (S) =SCULPEY

(TLS) =TRANSLUCENT LIQUID SCULPEY

**SOFT**    *quality before baking*    **HARD**

C — S — P — FS — F

**DURABLE**    *after baking*    **BRITTLE**

TLS—C—F—FS — P — S

**FLEXIBILITY**    *after baking*    **RIGIDITY**

TLS—F—FS—P — S—C

## BAKING TIME IS MORE SUBJECTIVE BUT IMPORTANT.

*How much baking time can the clay tolerate?*

S—C — P—TLS — FS—F

*as stated on the package*    *up to twice the time on the package*    *hours*

# Fimo

I have worked with Fimo for over 30 years. Fimo's unique combination of qualities inspired many of the techniques I've developed in polymer clay. These qualities are especially in evidence in my imitative techniques.

**Color**: Fimo offers a large palette of colors, from lightly to densely saturated pigments. This smorgasbord of available clays encourages customized mixing.

**Translucency/Opacity**: There's a wide range of opaque to translucent effects. White clay in Fimo is completely opaque and Art Translucent (#00) is quite translucent. By mixing colors carefully, you can get any color in any degree of translucency. Small round flecks are visible in the translucent and translucent-based clay mixtures after baking. Called pebbling or plaquing, this is the visible structure of the baked clay. This pebbling looks crystalline, aiding the re-creation of different stones and minerals.

**Stiffness**: Fimo is relatively stiff before baking. A variety of construction and assemblage techniques are possible that could not be done with a softer material. Although Fimo requires a bit more time and effort in conditioning, the effort is inconsequential compared to the possibilities that the workable stiffness affords for creating complex pieces.

**Durability/Multiple baking**: Fimo is very durable after baking. Opaque Fimo clay bodies can tolerate endless accumulated rebaking without color changes. When made into thin sheets, Fimo is slightly leathery after baking. This flexibility allows it to be bent or dropped without chipping and shattering.

**Fusability**: Fimo adheres to itself and other materials well before baking, and unlike other brands of clay, remains adhered well to itself after baking also. Fimo Soft may be gummy if the batch is bad, but in general Fimo is not inherently sticky or gummy to work with.

Fimo Soft is similar to Fimo Classic in the characteristics above. It is indeed softer than the Classic before baking, a result of extra plasiticizer in the clay body. But its range of colors and the names for those colors differ. For example, a beige-like color is called Champagne in Fimo Classic, but Sahara in Fimo Soft. Fimo Classic Champagne is a peachish-beige; the Fimo Soft Sahara is more of a grey-pink. Why take note of this? When imitating the visual effect of a material, precise color is very important.

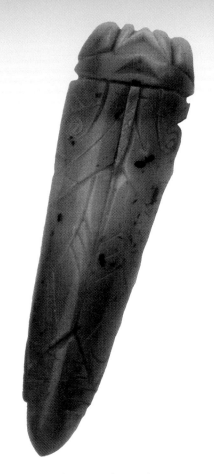

Victoria Hughes, *Beetle Pendants,* 1995. Fimo Art Translucent is responsible for the pebbly look of these imitative jade beetles. Prebaked inlays add color and metallic shimmer. The antennae are shaped and hammered brass wire. "Treat all surfaces evenly" is an ArtRanch adage, which means you should make the back of your pieces as beautiful as the front.

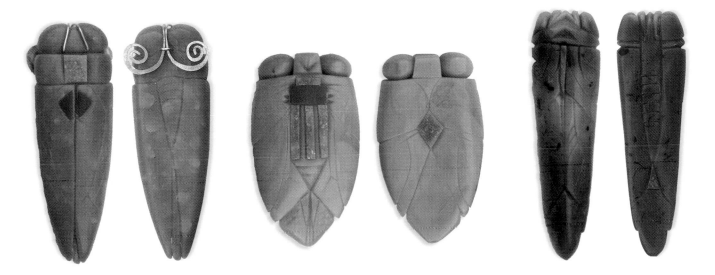

## Premo

Premo was developed by a group of polymer clay manufacturers in tandem with leading artists and teachers, in an admirably intelligent move to give the users of the material what they really want.

**Color**: A beautiful pure color range. Premo colors were selected specifically to act as "professional artists' colors." They were made to be mixed together just like paints to encourage artists to create their own colors from rich, densely pigmented clays.

**Translucency/Opacity**: Premo Translucent With Bleach is the most translucent of the different brands, sometimes labeled CFC06. Premo Translucent does not plaque. Its unobscured clarity allows you to create effects like agate, where translucent layering draws your eye into the depths of the material.

Premo also offers a lovely set of pearlescent and metallic clays in which small mica particles in the clay add sheen. Manipulation of these shimmering clays has spawned a whole group of magical and voluptuous effects. For instance, the micaceous sheen mimics the chatoyancy of tiger-eye beautifully.

**Stiffness**: Premo is softer and easier to manipulate before baking than Fimo. For many people this is the deciding factor in choosing Premo. However, Premo can become so soft that it is too gummy or sticky. If this occurs, press it between clean white sheets of paper overnight to leach some of the plasticizer out of the clay and thus stiffen it up. Or mix it with Fimo.

**Durability/Multiple baking**: Premo is not as durable as Fimo after baking, especially when used in sheets or as small-scale or linear elements. Chipping or breaking on corners can occur. If your pieces are primarily spherical, like beads or any other more stable shapes, you probably won't have a problem with this slight lack of durability. If you are making pages, slabs, linear elements, and the like, mix Premo with Fimo or Cernit for a stronger, more resilient clay body. Multiple bakings will gradually brown a Premo clay body.

**Fusability**: Premo does not fuse well to itself after baking and will tend to delaminate from other Premo layers, as well as from other polymer clays. To use it in any laminated techniques, you must mix it with other clays. Otherwise you will need to glue the layers with Zap-a-Gap or other cyanoacrylate glue after baking.

## Liquid Sculpey

Liquid Sculpey is another Polyform product that is definitely worth putting experimental time into. This fascinating and versatile material is not a modeling material, but a fluid form of polymer clay that can be handled in a variety of intriguing ways. It has the consistency of honey and is sold in squeeze bottles as well as in jars, so you can really play around. Its fluidity comes from a very high proportion of plasticizer in the polymer, so avoid prolonged skin contact or breathing the baking fumes. Translucent Liquid Sculpey, or TLS, is most translucent and most durable if baked on its own at 300°F, then laminated or glued to regular polymer clays, but it can be baked with other polymer clays at 275°F.

**Color**: Liquid Sculpey is manufactured in both a translucent version and an opaque version. Both can be tinted with dry pigments, acrylic paints, oil paints, and other media.

**Translucency/Opacity**: I only buy the TLS. I can make it opaque by adding a tiny drop of white acrylic paint to it. When baked on its own, without other polymer clays, TLS takes a higher temperature and really does become quite transparent, especially in thin sheets. For the imitative techniques, I often use TLS to reproduce a glazed effect on different materials like faience or porcelain.

**Stiffness**: When fresh, TLS has the consistency of honey. As it ages it becomes thicker and more viscous. Liquid Sculpey can be applied with a brush or finger (always use latex gloves so the plasticizer doesn't leach into your skin). If using a brush, just wrap the brush in aluminum foil between uses, as it is extremely difficult to clean. I usually apply Liquid Sculpey with my fingers for more control and to avoid getting air bubbles into the material.

**Durability/Multiple baking**: Liquid Sculpey is amazingly durable. When properly baked, TLS does not rip or tear, even when wadded up into a little ball or tugged, pulled, or stretched apart. It is often used as a coating and in thin sheets as well as delicate linear elements. I have used TLS for book covers and spines and been very satisfied with the resiliency it brings to the constantly stressed hinging sections. Other artists have even made garments out of TLS.

**Fusability**: Liquid Sculpey is so adherent it is used as an adhesive to fasten baked polymer clay together with unbaked polymer or with a baked polymer element. Apply a thin layer, press the piece to be adhered on top, and bake. For this purpose, bake the assembled clays at the temperature of the polymer clay, not the TLS. Baked TLS will not fuse especially well to unbaked polymers, though, and may need to be glued.

## Cernit

Cernit is a very useful polymer clay to have in your studio. I always use it in combination with other clays.

**Color**: Cernit offers an adequate range of colors, including pearlescent or "glamour" colors.

**Translucency/Opacity**: The clay body of Cernit tends to be rather translucent. This will be of benefit when you make amber, which is a luminous warm yellow. Dollmakers use Cernit extensively because the luminous, porcelain-like clay body creates a surface much like glowing human skin.

**Stiffness**: Before baking, Cernit can be quite soft, becoming gummy if overworked or in a warm environment. It also softens and slumps quite a bit during the baking process. For both these reasons, blend Fimo into Cernit to stiffen it and control the clay body before and during baking.

**Durability/Multiple baking**: Cernit is the most durable and rigid of all the clays after baking. When baked too long, too hot, or when rebaked, Cernit will change color, getting brown from prolonged exposure to heat. Therefore, Cernit is not suited for techniques requiring multiple baking.

**Fusability**: Cernit fuses well to itself and other polymers. Since it is a more durable material on its own, joints between Cernit and other materials will be stronger.

Despite these challenges, Cernit has such a major advantage in post-baking rigidity and durability over other brands that I always have some on hand to mix with other brands before baking. I mix Cernit and Fimo to increase the translucency of a Fimo clay body without diluting its color saturation. I also mix Cernit into the clay body to add rigidity.

## storing mixed clay

Polymer clay does not dry out. It is, however, affected by heat, direct sunlight, and airborne dust and contaminants. The clay needs to be kept covered and away from heat. I keep my mixed colors on my worktable, covered with Saran Wrap. I've found that this brand of plastic wrap is unaffected by the plasticizer in the clay. Other people keep their clays in plastic storage boxes or between sheets of wax paper in boxes. If you're not going to use the clays for several weeks, seal them in double plastic bags and store them in the freezer.

When putting the clay in contact with other plastics, be careful that the polymer clay is not melting the other plastic. Cheap plastics are most susceptible to the plasticizer. You'll know after a day. I once stored clays overnight on inexpensive plastic take-out food trays. The next morning, I picked up a conditioned clay ball from the tray and long strings of gooey melted plastic stretched up from the bottom of the clay like chewing gum.

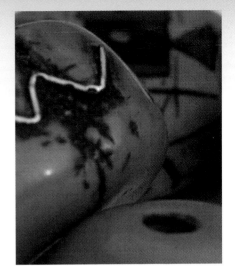

Victoria Hughes, *Amber Beads,* 1996. The luminosity of these amber beads comes from Cernit in the mix. The hammered wire w-shape in the large bead at left is a traditional North African repair of amber beads, which have been valued for millennia and are treated with love. The bead caps on the larger bead in the back are polymer imitating silver. Shortened carpet tacks ring the larger reddish copal bead on the right.

## prebaked inlays

Just as it sounds, these are prebaked elements of polymer clay that are made thin specifically to be inlaid into unbaked clay and baked again. Most Fimo, Prēmo, and TLS elements can be rebaked. All are made as larger sheets, tubes, and canes. After they are finished, they can be cut up on demand for specific projects.

Start a collection of baked thin sheets, canes, and small molded decorations that you can use in your designs to quickly add defined areas of color and pattern.

Victoria Hughes, *Pendants,* 1995. These house pendants are all made of Fimo and combine prebaked imitative inlays with different textures and molded elements. For instance, the small bird is a molded version of an original referring to Peruvian spindle-whorl designs. The blue half circles are cross sections of a lapis tube, bisected to create an arc.

## acrylic paints

Acrylic paints and polymer clays are like good business partners: they have compatible but not identical interests and abilities and they work well together on a wide range of projects. Get to know their possibilities.

Acrylics extend the range of possibilities available to polymer clay. A form of polymer themselves, they are completely compatible with the clays. They are produced in an enormous range of colors, opacities, viscosities, textural qualities, and metallic and pearlescent effects. They can be used on top of the clay, between clay layers, and mixed into the clay body itself. Used before or after baking, they are as versatile as the clay. They become permanently fused onto the polymer after baking.

Different brands have varying qualities. Variations primarily occur in density and purity of pigment, opacity and translucency, viscosity, and adhesion to the underlying materials. Sound like a familiar list? Exactly: it's the same set of qualities as the polymer clays.

Experiment with different brands and see which you prefer. Keep samples in your logbook just as you do with clay samples, creating a personalized reference library. There is much more variation between paint brands than you may expect. For the imitative techniques, which demand specific pigments, adhesion, and opacities, I use primarily Liquitex and Golden Artists Colors.

Liquitex is easy to find, inexpensive, and workable. Liquitex is especially appropriate for antiquing baked polymer clay pieces. Antiquing requires a certain amount of fussing, and fortunately this paint allows a lot of fussing because of its slower adherence to the polymer's surface and its lower saturation of pigment. It's a good basic line of paint for any studio.

Golden Artists Colors makes a high-quality paint designed for professional artists. Their paints are wonderful. I use Golden paints for thin washes or tinting on the clay and for literally painting on baked imitative pieces. The paints adhere to the clay immediately and are richly and densely pigmented in an enormous range of unusual and seductive effects.

Golden Artists Colors developed the interference paints, which have an opaline shimmer and dichroic sheen that epitomize both the ancient luster of buried glass and the futuristic look of light caught in another space and time. The company also has a large line of coatings, lacquers, and textured media worth getting to know. Golden loves to work with artists to create specialized, unique paints. Several of the paints and materials now available in their line arose from such customized formulae that Golden brought into the commercial realm.

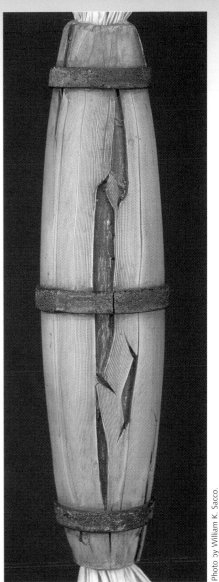

Photo by William K. Sacco.

Diane Villano, *Bound Ivory Bead,* detail, 2001. Effective and unusual handling of paint on this fragmented imitative ivory bead accents its intriguing surface textures.

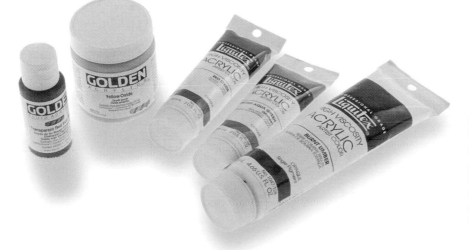

Different brands of acrylic paints, like brands of polymer, have different characteristics. Liquitex and Golden Artists Colors work well for the imitative techniques, supplying a wide range of color, opacity, texture, saturation of pigment, and adherence to the clay's surface.

Jacqueline Lee, *Peony Pendant*, 2001. Precise use of metallic powders, both dabbed on the peony and also mixed into the black clay body, beautifully conjure the antique metals that this inro evokes.

Photo by Don Haab.

## metallic surface effects

One of the imitative techniques imitates metals. It's almost entirely a surface affair. The illusion is created with a variety of metallic powders, paints, and patinas that in combination give a realistic deep luster to create the look of silver, gold, copper, steel, and bronze.

Metallic powders are used as an undercoating, primarily as a release agent. I use Pearl-Ex and Fimo Pulver powders for this.

Metallic waxes such as Treasure Gold add a delicate highlighting across the top of a painted metallic piece. These waxes will dry out over time, so keep some mineral oil around and put a drop in the small tub when they are getting so stiff you can't control them easily.

Additional metallic effects layer metallic paints over the powders and even mix powders into the paints to augment the metallic luster. An increasing assortment of the patinas and surface treatments available in craft and art stores are compatible with polymer clay and can be layered with these techniques. When in doubt, experiment. Have fun with all the options offered.

## wire

When it comes to making rigid, linear elements, polymer clay needs a little support from wire. Wire is a fascinating material—a thin, flexible, coherent thread made from something usually encountered as a solid mass. Wire is carefully manufactured and is a sophisticated technical accomplishment, although it is so ubiquitous it has become nearly invisible in our culture, similar to the place plastic has created for itself. Imagine a world without plastic. Or wire. Hmmm.

There are both precious and nonprecious metal wires, a large range of colors in the nonprecious wire, a range of gauges in all wire, wire that "remembers" how it was curled, wire that's wrapped with other wire or with colored or clear nylon sheathing, wire that is stiff and resilient, wire that is soft and reformable … the list goes on and on, offering a myriad of choices.

For imitative techniques, I use silver, nickel silver, or brass wire in specific sizes between 12- to 20-gauge. Primarily I use 18-gauge for the projects in this book. The gauge refers to the diameter of the wire: the higher the number, the

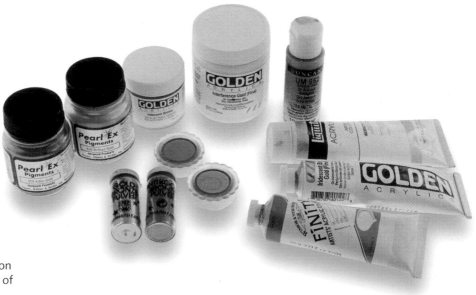

The more metallics, the richer they look! Mix and blend powders, add powders to paints, layer waxes and patinas over paints. Accumulate a buildup of different metallic effects on the polymer to generate the illusion of a true metallic object.

finer the wire. Thus, 12-gauge wire is thicker and stiffer than 22-gauge wire of the same material.

All three metals are soft and easy to manipulate, especially in smaller sizes. Most cultures that use the materials mimicked in this book use silver wire or occasionally brass wire. For realism, I've used the same for the projects in the book. As always, though, experiment on your own to determine what pleases you most. Remember that the point of the imitative techniques is not to fool others but to master polymer clay as a material, and thus have the control to fabricate your personal vision.

Silver wire can be work-hardened–made stiffer by hammering or bending. Silver-plated wire will be as soft or stiff as the interior wire. Nickel silver–an alloy of copper, zinc, and nickel–is naturally stiffer than pure silver. Sterling silver is 92.5% silver and 7.5% copper. Both silver and nickel silver tarnish and this slight blackening can be enhanced with chemicals to add a sense of antiquity.

Gold-colored wire nicely accents imitative materials. Brass wire is an easily formable wire

Victoria Hughes, *Turquoise Choker*, 2002. Hammered silver spirals function both as embellishment and as the carrier for the necklace cord on this imitative turquoise choker.

made of copper and zinc. Brass wire can be used for armatures as well as for external decor elements and is inexpensive and pliable. Brass takes hammered textures nicely. It will tarnish, so either coat the wire or accept the aged look that the inevitable patina brings to your piece. Gold-plated wire is more expensive but will not tarnish.

### note

*When cutting wire, keep the end to be cut off aimed down toward your work surface or lap. Be very careful of where the cut piece will go. Cutting wire sends the sharp cut piece off like an arrow. You must control where it is goes. Be attentive and aware. If the wire hits someone in the eye, it can cause major injury.*

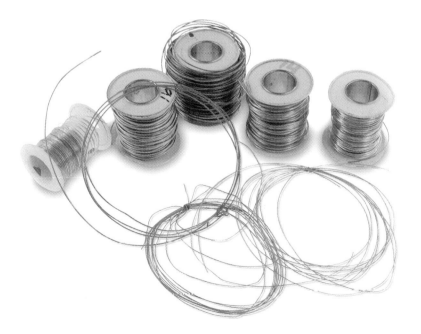

Jewelry supply stores carry a variety of wire gauges and metals. Gold and silver wire is usually sold by the inch or foot, and brass, nickel silver, copper, brass, and other more common metals are available on a spool. The wires pictured range in diameter from 14- to 20-gauge.

This category includes finer materials to be added into or rubbed onto the surface of your piece. At the ArtRanch, I have vials of different earths and sands that I've gathered on my travels to rub onto or into my pieces. Look around your own site and collect what interests you, then try these in different settings and see how you like them. Look for anything you might add into the clay body or apply on the surface of your piece.

Earth and other retrieved materials add a great deal to the visual and tactile realism of the imitative techniques. I use the term "retrieved materials" to indicate anything you brought from a different context to use in your art-making processes. This category includes what Americans call dirt and Canadians call earth. It also includes dust, sand, spices, herbs, and grits used for abrasion–basically any fine particulate or fiber that you can mix into or apply onto your pieces.

Many evocative old surfaces have accumulated layers of substances. Some objects have had oils, waxes, animal fat, blood, and other materials deliberately applied to them. In mimicking time itself, dust and dirt are subtle but important components.

Victoria Hughes, *Vessels*, 2001. I mixed rosemary into translucent clay, then formed the clay into these small vessels in an experiment aiming at jasper. I used wire hoops to fasten the apple branches to the taller form. I baked the upper sections of both vessels first to preserve their precise contours, then attached them to the lower unbaked polymer forms and baked again.

Often a subtle hand-rubbed layer of dry clay or fine dust is the quintessential touch to transform your piece into a compelling object. Pictured here is a potpourri of different materials–earths, ashes, spices, rock salt, tiny pebbles–that can be added in or on your polymer clay pieces. Larger rocks are forms for bowls, like the black bowl in the background holding bark chips used for texturing amber. Rocks also can serve as armatures for some sculptures, encased permanently in polymer. The world around you gives forth these materials: gather the elements that attract you.

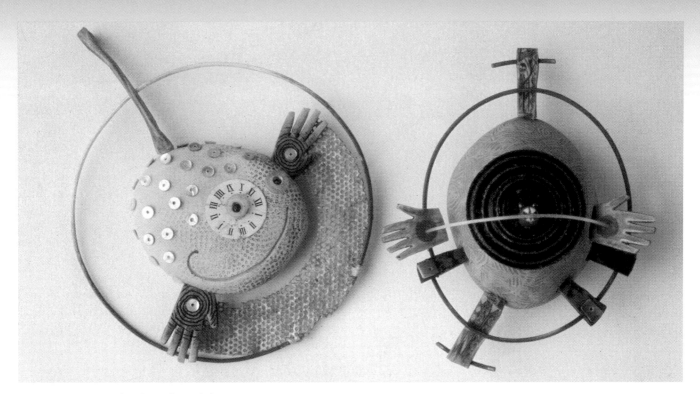

For instance, the fine dry adobe earth in the Southwest is a good all-around addition to any imitative sandstone, ceramic, or dusty material. Soft clean ashes from your fireplace can be used, as well as brick dust; whatever you personally sense might be interesting. These different particulates are applied over wet acrylic paint, which will hold them on the polymer.

The organic materials listed above–spices, herbs, and the like–are used primarily in the clay body itself, often mixed into a translucent clay through which their textures and colors are visible. Pepper adds a small crystalline black and white flecking to faux granite, curry powder gives a lovely uneven saffron/ochre coloring similar to some jaspers and petrified wood. Fine salt rolled on the surface of unbaked clay creates an angular grainy texture with a nicely pitted, corroded feel to it, which develops after baking when you rinse the salt off.

Look around you and keep trying things, and you'll find the universe provides all sorts of intriguing materials to complement your work.

Victoria Hughes, *Bound by Time, Bound by Speech,* 1995. These two sculptures examine how we bind up our creativity. Polymer clay baked over rocks: the surface has been textured and augmented, pale ash has been rubbed into the baked surface texture, and other polymer and nonpolymer elements have been glued onto the pieces. Basketry reeds loop around "Time," and baked polymer hands span a found aluminum piece. Heavy nylon cord from a weed cutter is clenched in the very sharp, very tiny teeth of "Speech," whose face is an old metal button back. Zap-a-Gap adheres the various media to the baked polymer.

## found objects

This category covers anything you might add or adhere onto the surface of your polymer clay pieces. Some examples are pictured to stimulate your creativity but other than feathers and a few small interesting objects to make molds, the projects in this book will not require them.

I have baskets and drawers of materials, objects, bits and pieces of this and that, a bag of feathers, a case of beetle wings, a drawer of snakeskin and fur, a box of Braille pages, stones, feathers, paper, photographs and other ephemera, glass, old jewelry pieces, small nails and other hardware store goodies, fishing pieces, rusted metal objects, fabric, lace, ribbon, plastic bits, and lots more. Many of these things pertain to polymer clay and mixed media art generally. Remember that anything you find attractive can be included somehow in your polymer clay artwork, as inspiration or as an additional component.

Go forage, collect what excites you, keep things reasonably organized, and you'll find that the delight of discovering these things will inform your imagination.

Almost any material can tolerate the baking temperature, so polymer's application to mixed media projects ranges indiscriminately far and wide. Early plastics are the only exceptions: Bakelite, celluloid, and contemporary inexpensive plastics deform and melt in the baking temperatures, as do objects that have pitch or asphaltum in them.

Organic materials dry out when heated. Use them in your designs but know they will change. Materials like leaves will turn brown and become very brittle. Bones will become brittle and lose their springiness. Feathers fare well in general, although they also become slightly more brittle. Certain types of beetle wings change color slightly as the heat changes the physical structure of the iridescent surface.

## glue

Stirring up interest and controversy since the beginning, "what glue to use" is the big question. Early jewelers no doubt murmured, "Hmm, feathers to shells, what glue to use, honey or that sticky red mud?"

There are two types of glue here at the ArtRanch—Sobo, and Zap-a-

One of polymer clay's delightful quirks is its ability to get along with everything and everybody. Due to the low baking temperature, almost any material can be incorporated into your design. Here, an evocative assemblage of items from the hardware store, the fabric store, the beach, the side of the road, antique dealers, pet stores, abandoned industrial sites... All meant to coax you into accepting the gift of your own aesthetic choices. There are no bad found objects.

Gap. Glue choice depends on the properties of the elements to be adhered to the clay: are they porous or nonporous? The basic concept is to assemble everything together before baking, bake, then lift up and glue back down the things that did not fuse to the clay.

Use Sobo, a type of white glue, to glue porous materials to polymer. Porous materials include paper, fibers, feathers, wood, fabric, thin leathers and suedes, and other materials that would be affected by water. Sobo and other white glues are PVA glues, which are chemically related to PVC, so the glue and clay are quite compatible. They are water-soluble glues. I prefer Sobo to the other brands because it is stronger and more flexible.

To glue nonporous materials to polymer clay, use Zap-a-Gap or Slo-Zap, a cyanoacrylate glue like Super Glue. Nonporous materials include metal and wire, stone, glass, other plastics including pre-baked polymer clay elements, and other materials that are not affected by water. Except for the plastics, none of these materials will fuse to the polymer clay dur-

ing baking, so will need to be glued afterwards.

Slo-Zap is a thicker, slightly more viscous version of Zap-a-Gap. Its 10-second setup time allows gluing of delicate elements or objects that may need repositioning, like hinges or pin backs.

## lacquer and varnish

For the most part, imitative pieces are not lacquered, they are sanded and polished. The lustrous beauty of natural materials comes from the patina developed on the surface over time: either when objects were handled through the years, or when the objects were sanded and polished during their manufacture. Deeper areas of these objects or materials are matte, sometimes a little dusty.

Lacquer spreads an even glossy shine over the entire area lacquered, including the deeper areas, and is entirely contradictory in effect to the subtle, natural surface sheen we are after. Resist the temptation to lacquer an entire imitative object, like a jade bead or a coral branch. It will look wrong.

However, in three special cases lacquer is an appropriate surface coat on the imitative pieces: for protecting indigo transfers and other delicate surface treatments, to shine isolated elements that will contrast with a surrounding matte imitative material, and to shine areas that the buffing wheel cannot reach.

For protective coatings on delicate surfaces, I use Golden Varnishes brand Polymer Varnish with UVLS. I buy the matte formula and have discovered that it is possible to buff the surface a bit to bring up a sheen on the higher areas, as would occur naturally.

For a durable high shine on small inlays, interiors of bowls, or other specific areas needing a glossy finish, I use Fimo Gloss Varnish, the solvent-based glossy lacquer made for Fimo by Eberhard Faber. Often I put on a few drops and quickly smear it evenly over the surface, then let it dry. This gives a more matte surface as well. Buy the lacquer in the small bottles and use the brushes that come in those caps (the varnish is very difficult to clean out of brushes). Buy large jars to refill the small bottles.

I am often asked, "What glue do you use?" Many different glues are available and there are almost as many different ideas about what works best. The glues, lacquers, and varnishes here are simple to work with and have worked well for years.

## a note about epoxies

*Epoxies will work in areas where there is no stress on the bond working to peel it apart. Some jewelers use it to glue on pin backs and have not had a problem. Epoxy, however, does not establish a fused, permanent bond with polymer clay. Use it selectively. For your creative designs and way of working, it may be a successful option.*

 tools

Basic hand-operated tools for polymer clay. From the top: a pasta machine for making flat sheets of polymer, a straight-sided drinking glass also used for flattening polymer, an assortment of brushes both for painting and for pushing paint into deeper indentations, a nonserrated knife for moving unbaked pieces, tissue blades, a quartet of pliers, an X-acto knife with a shallow-angled number #19 blade, two linoleum blades in polymer handles, two drill bits also mounted in polymer handles, and below a regular hammer, a steel plate to hammer against, and a checkering file to pattern baked polymer.

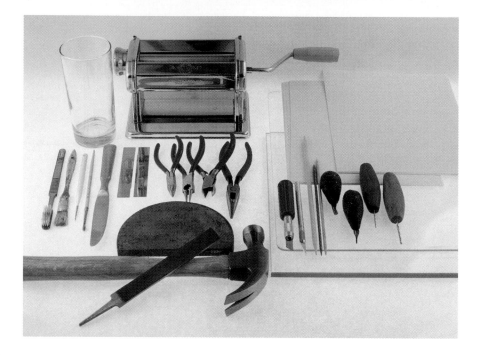

your hands
work surfaces, including
    paper
pasta machine
drinking glass
scraper/knife
knitting needles
paintbrushes
X-acto knife
tissue blade
texturing and embossing
    tools
carving tools
drills
pliers
wire cutters
vessel forms
sandpaper
food processor or food
    chopper
oven
buffer
sander
safety equipment

The imitative techniques can be done with very simple tools. Most of these tools are hand-operated and have probably already accumulated in your toolbox. Having access to a few basic power tools for the finishing techniques will quickly give you those evocative surfaces. The quality of your tools always makes a huge difference in the ease of work, and therefore in how quickly and directly you can bring your idea into existence. This is another category whose contents will change as you personalize your ways of working.

### your hands

The first, most important tools for everything you do in your life are your hands. Magnificent, extremely versatile, and hypersensitive, these intelligent meta-tools are you, a physical extension of your mind that can manipulate matter. They participate in an ongoing positive feedback loop of information, action, and control. You got your hands for free as part of your human birthright. You could never find tools like these at a hardware store.

Whenever you have a chance to put your hands on something, to affect it or gauge it, do so. Touching gives you direct information about a material, data not available from way up there near your eyeballs. This is why I suggest conditioning by hand rather than using too many tools (to be able to accurately gauge the clay's consistency) and why I advocate using a glass to flatten the clay rather than a pasta machine. Your hands give you complete control over the results of your actions: a tool always has its own margin of error built in.

Respect your hands, use them, take care of them and be thankful for human handedness.

## work surfaces, including paper

The best work surface is smooth and nonsticky. Glass, glazed tiles, and tempered glass cutting boards are all acceptable. Transparent work surfaces allow you to see grids or patterns on paper under the work surface. I use pieces of glass, 12" to 16" square and 1/4" thick with sanded edges. I keep several in the studio for different projects under construction at one time. I also have several 6" glass squares, small enough to set in the oven. These are especially useful for working with TLS.

Stay away from clear plastic sheet of all types. It scratches easily and the polymer sticks to the scratches. Some types are affected by the plasticizer in the polymer and degrade over time. Although clear plastic sheets are lightweight, they are not unbreakable.

Working directly on pieces of paper allows you to avoid distorting your piece when moving it from the work surface to the oven. Baking parchment or white copy paper works for this, although parchment is easier to peel away from your pieces. I use recycled paper such as the back side of old photocopies, being very careful never ever to lay the unbaked clay on the photocopy side of the paper, as the image will transfer (that's a technique!).

Whatever type of work surface you use, keep it clean and organ-ized enough to be easy and inviting to work on. Don't allow clutter to decrease the size of your work area, and thus decrease the potential size of your art.

Photo by Daniel Neal.

Dayle Doroshow, *Golden Plumb Bob,* 1999. The antique, totemic impact of this piece arises from transfers under translucent clay, sanded, polished, and painted. An exciting contrast of forms, as the rigid linearity of the brass wire spirits up and out of the drop.

Work surfaces. Glass is best. Plain white paper can be used under polymer clay when making and baking pieces. Grid paper is handy for measuring and construction and can be slid under the glass or you may work directly on it.

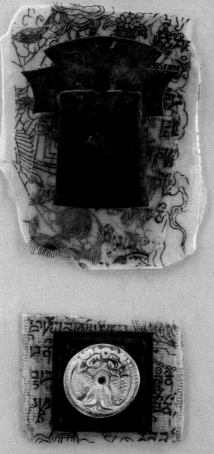

Gwen Gibson, *Wall Piece,* 1996. Varying the thickness of layers of thin sheets of polymer, each one worked differently, increases the voluptuous tactile appeal of this wall piece. Painting, transfers, patinas: a host of rich, expressive surfaces are Gibson's trademark.

Photo by Robert Diamante.

## drinking glass

This is the all-around most necessary tool for polymer clay other than the oven. A clear, straight-sided drinking glass, with no taper from top to bottom, is the best rolling tool for polymer clay. Place one hand on each side of the glass, then look through it to monitor your work. All rolling is completely controlled, and as simple and direct as possible.

Because it's glass, it's easy to keep clean. Because it is a glass, you automatically stand it up when not using it so it never rolls off the table. A clear bud vase will work well also but its narrower diameter and greater curvature will distort the surface of your work a bit, making it harder to see what you are doing.

## pasta machine

Pasta machines are useful but not vital for the imitative techniques. The most common pasta machine is made by Atlas, an Italian company. It has seven settings, from #1 for the thickest to #7 for the thinnest sheet. Other brands of pasta machines exist, including some with nine settings and one whose numbering system runs the other way, so that #1 is the thinnest setting. All, obviously, only extrude sheets of the thickness of different types of pasta.

Pasta machines have two heavy steel rollers that roll toward each other when a crank is turned on the side. These flatten anything that comes between them and extrude it below the rollers. The rollers are durable, but will pit if something hard and grainy, like sand, is run through with the polymer clay. Once the rollers themselves are textured, they will emboss that texture onto every subsequent sheet of clay.

Pasta machines clamp onto your worktable and are easy to use. They are moderately easy to keep clean with cleansing wipes. Do not take a pasta machine apart to clean it: it's virtually impossible to get it together again.

Additional attachments are available for these machines. There are rollers that shred the clay (or pasta) into long threads (spaghetti). There is even an attachable motor so you don't have to turn the crank to roll the clay through. I have a basic pasta machine, which I use primarily for making flat sheets for imitation agates and for flat pages, postcards, and book elements.

Do not use any tool or appliance for both food and polymer clay. The plasticizer in the polymer clays is not healthy to ingest, and contact between food and the plasticizer must be avoided. Tools for polymer must be dedicated to this use only. Do not make noodles with this machine in your spare time!

Rumor has it that the American polymer clay community is legendary in the Italian pasta-machine industry for its demand for these versatile tools. Pasta machines like this classic Atlas roll out endlessly even sheets of clay, and create some spectacular effects for other nonimitative techniques.

## scraper/knife

Often while working you'll need to lift your current piece to move it, add elements, and adjust it. A steel rib or knife of some sort accomplishes this. I use an old dinner knife with the serrations filed off. It is a perfect wedge, ideal for separating polymer from the work surface. The handle makes the tapered blade easy to manipulate and the blade easily slides under the clay piece to be lifted and wedges it up.

To use it, slip it under the piece with the tip of the blade protruding past the edge of the piece. Press the blade down on your work surface and slide it across, under the clay to be lifted. Your action is wedging rather than slicing, which would remove the back of the piece. Don't use tissue blades for this action.

Steel ribs are semicircles of steel used in ceramics that can be used for scrapers. Palette knives will work in a pinch. However, the edges of both tools have a blunt cross section rather than a tapered edge and, as the edge shoves against the edge of your clay piece, it can distort the piece as it pushes its way beneath.

## knitting needles

Metal knitting needles have many applications in the studio. The smooth metal is easy to keep clean and does not interact with the plasticizer. The imitative techniques use knitting needles primarily for making holes in beads. Get one or two that are slightly bigger than the cord you will be using to string your beads.

Knitting needles have many other applications. They can be used to emboss round and conical patterns onto unbaked clay. They can be inserted inside a tube of clay and used as a handle to roll the clay tube over a texture, or

rolled inside a cone of clay to expand it gradually, or used to form long straight tubes for hinges and other cylindrical adventures. Polymer clay tubes can be baked directly on a knitting needle, eliminating the distortion that occurs when moving unbaked clay forms.

## paintbrushes

For the imitative techniques, you'll need a stiff brush to poke paint down into deep, narrow crevices. A stencil or tole painting brush works well for this, as does an old toothbrush. Most paint application on surfaces will be done with your fingers. A good brush for painting controlled patterns and edging paint into incised lines will be useful too.

In these techniques you will use acrylic paints. Keep the brushes rinsed out. Acrylic paint dries quickly and permanent. It's possible to ruin a nice brush in less than an hour if the paint dries completely on the bristles.

## X-acto knife and tissue blade

Use an X-acto knife with a #19 blade. This blade ends in a shallower angle and is more versatile for the techniques in this book. The #19 blade fits into a bigger, more comfortable handle that is more controllable than the slender handle of the acutely angled blades.

Because this blade is shallower, your hand can fit under the handle when the cutting edge of the blade is parallel to the table. This allows you to cut small, precise shapes from baked sheets and to emboss careful lines and angles onto unbaked polymer. I keep several blades handy, one of which is deliberately dulled so that embossing with it leaves a line rather than a slice.

The tissue blade is a thin, supple steel rectangle about 1" by 6" with a sharpened edge running the length of one side. This tool was introduced to the polymer clay community by Nan Roche, an

Nonserrated dinner knives and potters' steel ribs let you lift up unbaked pieces as you are working. This particular knife has been with me for 20 years. My father ground the serrations from one of our family knives, sanded the edge of the blade down, and made a perfect tool. Thanks, dad.

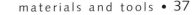

Above: Victoria Hughes, *Guardian Pendants,* 1993. These protective beasties with the hinged jaws announce themselves loudly, but the technical process for making them is equally clear. The external shapes were cut with a bowed tissue blade and all the patterning was embossed before baking, using tools like the flat of the point of the X-acto knife, the tip of a needle tool, and a ribbon-wire spiral.

artist and the author of *The New Clay,* who is a scientist by profession. We are indebted to her: it's hard to imagine working with polymer clay without tissue blades.

The tissue blade is used for a wide range of cutting, slicing, and shaping actions. Its suppleness allows you to bend it in a beautiful arc, and cut that arc by pressing straight down through your clay. Its thinness allows perfect, beautifully thin slices through the clay. Keep several on hand.

Although the blade is steel, the cutting edge is very thin and sharp and prone to being nicked by cutting through other materials. The blades also will discolor or rust over time. When this happens, sand them with 600-grit sandpaper to help maintain the cutting surface longer. Some artists dab brightly colored nail polish along the unsharpened edge of the blade, so when they grab it and start cutting, they always know which side is sharp.

Tissue blades and X-acto knives are indispensable items in the toolbox. The wide, shallow X-acto #19 blade with the red handle makes possible types of cuts and processes that the more acute blade does not. Always have an extra tissue blade for backup.

## molds, texturing and embossing tools

For controlled and predictable embossed patterns, polymer clay takes textures so beautifully that almost everything will work in this category. Different types of sandpapers and other abrasive media indent unbaked polymer in rough-edged random textural areas.

Dragon skin is an abrasive for removing old paint layers from floors. It creates a pattern of small circles. When pressed upside down into the polymer, small perfect raised dots appear. You are most likely to find dragon skin at old-style hardware stores.

Try texturing with anything that catches your eye. One of my favorite texturing tools is a piece of broken headlight reflector. Industrially milled into thousands of tiny and exact pyramids, the shining plastic embosses a precise pattern of triangles deep enough to be filled with a contrasting color of clay and rebaked, or just highlighted with paint. What's around you that will create a wonderful texture in the clay?

Mold-making and use is a huge category unto itself. For the imitative techniques, the basics will be enough. Well-conditioned unbaked polymer clay, liberally coated with cornstarch or another mold release agent, will faithfully copy any texture or relief that it is pressed against. Bake this and a perfect polymer clay mold will result. Some of my favorite molds are flat pads into which I have carved designs after baking. Almost all my molds are made from polymer clay, because it takes an impression or a carving so easily.

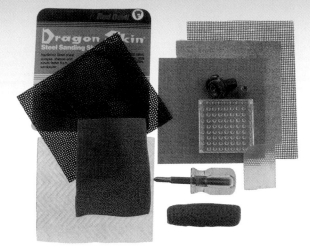

Although virtually anything will texture unbaked polymer clay, the materials shown here are particularly applicable to the imitative techniques. Coarse sandpapers, dragon skin, intriguingly-shaped tools, found textures like a rubber floor mat, and fabricated molds and embossing surfaces all work well.

Sheila Miller, *Wall Piece,* 1998. Dragon skin and a number of other interesting found textures and objects were embossed into this wall piece and the expressive surface embellished with polymer and nonpolymer elements. Rough, torn edges are easy to get with Fimo, and accentuate the sense here of an ancient fragment.

Photo by Robert E. Miller

## carving tools

The tools made for carving linoleum printing blocks are ideal to carve designs in baked polymer. I use them to incise my pieces, to create embossing surfaces, and to carve my logo on the back of finished pieces. Speedball makes a good basic line of carving blades. They come in a v-shaped and a u-shaped style, and in large and small sizes. Get one of each.

I find the commercially available handles do not fit my hand or offer the control I like, so I make my own handles. To do so, make an egg-shaped ball of unbaked clay that feels balanced in your grip, and insert the steel carving blade into the clay. Pinch the clay tight to the base of the carving blade and bake. After baking, pull the blade out, put Zap-a-Gap on it, and reinsert it. If the blade loosens, just pull it out, sand any old glue off the steel, rough the metal with a file or rasp, reglue, and reinsert it.

Victoria Hughes, *Fish Amulet,* 1995, collection Robert Liu. Lapis inlays in the eyes accentuate the pale translucent jade green. Carved scales are pointed up by a light ivory paint in the deeper grooves. The central section is a shell that slides up and off the inner fish body, revealing an interior cavity full of herringbones.

Above: Polymer clay is surprisingly easy to carve and model after baking. Carving can be used both for direct relief patterning and to create embossing plates. Speedball makes small and large v-shaped and u-shaped blades. Make your own handle for the blade for the most control and comfort when carving.

## drills

Hand drilling is often used in working baked polymer clay. Because of the ease of working baked polymer, electric drills are not necessary. In fact, their speed and friction bites into the clay

Right: Hand drills work best with polymer, since the clay is relatively workable even after baking. As with linoleum cutters, mount the drill bits in polymer clay handles that fit your hand, and glue the bit securely after baking. A jeweler's or watchmaker's pin vise is easiest to use for the smaller bits.

quickly, making control of drilling difficult.

As with carving tools, I buy drill bits in several sizes and mount them in polymer handles. The smaller drill bits from hardware stores are useful sizes for polymer sculpture. Augment that selection with jewelry-scale drill bits for rotary electric drills like Dremel tools. Smaller bits will create holes corresponding to the gauges of wire used for earrings and other jewelry. Larger bits flesh out the assortment for those random creative projects that come up. As you develop your personal style, you will know which sizes suit your way of working.

## pliers

For the imitative techniques, you'll need two or three pairs of pliers: needle-nose, round-nose, and cutting pliers. The needle-nose or round-nose pliers may have a cutting surface close to the hinge at the back.

If you are going to do much wire work, consider investing in good-quality tools. Inexpensive tools can be difficult to control and are hard on your hands.

## vessel forms

Polymer clay bowls and vessels show off imitative techniques

Victoria Hughes, *Imitative Vessels,* 1995. Thin sheets of unbaked polymer clay can be eased over vessel forms and baked. The uncomplicated shape of the turquoise bowl derives from a large stainless steel soup ladle whose handle I filed off. The ivory and amber vessels were fabricated from tubes and baked in stages to preserve their hollow cylindrical forms.

nicely. A vessel form is any object over which you can cast a vessel or elements of a vessel. Since the clay is pressed over the outside surface of the form, that outer surface will be embossed on the inside of your polymer vessel. Glass or metal forms will leave a smooth, sometimes glassy interior to the bowl.

Rougher surfaces like rocks will emboss a matte surface texture.

Release agents are not needed for these projects because the polymer does not fuse to the glass, metal, or stone during baking. However, it will fuse to any paint or lacquer coating on the glass or metal, making removal of the form impossible. Sand the forms clean.

Many stainless-steel vessel forms can be found in cooking or restaurant supply stores. The lighting supply sections of large hardware stores often have lamp parts and bases that serve well (sand the varnish or paint off the metal first). Recycled light bulbs are perfect forms for small hemispherical bowls.

Polymer vessels are cast on the outside of volumetric forms. A good vessel form is one that is glass or bare metal and has a smooth surface that opens out continuously.

## sandpaper

A necessary first step for polishing baked polymer, sanding can also be a tool to refine the shape of baked clay.

Sandpapers are identified by the size and type of grit deposited on the paper. Some are made of waterproof materials and designed to be used in water: these wet-or-dry sandpapers are the type used in the imitative techniques.

Higher numbers on sandpaper indicates finer grits, which smooth more than they abrade. Lower numbers are coarser grits that abrade more than they smooth. Hardware stores carry 80-grit to 400- or 600-grit sandpapers. Sandpapers above 600-grit are available at auto parts stores only (they're used for sanding automobile repairs).

For various texturing applications before baking, keep a range of regular (not wet-or-dry) sandpapers on hand, starting with the very rough 80- and 100-grit sandpapers, which emboss matte textures onto unbaked clay. Drywall sandpaper, an open mesh coated in carbide grit, textures the unbaked polymer in a coarse-edged screen pattern.

For sanding applications after baking, get at least one sheet each of wet-or-dry sandpaper in grits of 220-, 320-, 400-, 600-, and 900- or 1000. Purchase a sanding sponge to wrap the sandpaper around so your hands don't become sore from clutching tightly onto thin pieces of sandpaper.

Sandpapers have many applications in the world of polymer clay. Wet-or-dry sandpaper gives that lusciously smooth surface that characterizes most of the imitative techniques. The horizontal belt sander can use Trizact belts, which are designed for plastics, and leave a smoother surface than woodworkers' sanding belts.

Now let's open the cabinet with the power tools. Grab an extension cord and follow me. Of course you are reading the manufacturer's safety instructions, right? Always follow proper safety guidelines around power tools. These work well because they are very powerful. Channel that power toward your project, not toward your body.

## food processor or food chopper

Food processors chop up the polymer clay into small nuggets, and also soften the clay slightly as the blade friction heats up the polymer. For re-creating turquoise, you'll need at least a small food chopper to generate the right consistency of clay. Food processors also can be helpful in the conditioning process.

As with the pasta machine, get a food processor or chopper that you use only for polymer clay. The machine itself need not be fancy or expensive, but be very careful

Nan Roche, *Brooch*, 2002. Very thin layers of lacquer-like colored clay were embossed and sanded away, and the resulting brushy effect of the irregularly removed clay suggests age and complexity.

Photo by the artist.

with smaller choppers not to overheat the motor and burn it out. Polymer clay is thick and heavy, challenging for the chopper to work through. Running too much clay at once or not letting the motor rest every 10 minutes or so will shorten the life of the smaller machines considerably.

The plastic basket needs to be cleaned periodically by washing off the plasticizer film or using a solvent of some sort. If a film of plasticizer is left on the plastic, it will deteriorate the basket. The basket will craze, get sticky, be hard to clean, and crack easily. Then you'll have to track down a new basket, which takes time away from your art. It's much easier to clean the basket occasionally instead.

Use a dry paper towel between uses to wipe the smallest clay nuggets from the basket, the blades, and the cover. These small polymer clay pieces cling because of static, and should be removed to avoid mixing colors. This is especially important when using the processor to generate nuggets to be baked as is (random bright-orange clay nuggets in your turquoise will look wrong).

## oven

Ah, the oven—the only absolutely necessary tool for polymer clay. You must have an oven that will heat evenly and precisely and that will hold 275°F consistently for hours. Its worth depends on maintaining that consistent temperature throughout the volume of air.

Toaster ovens tend to be good, mostly because they are so small there are no cold spots. Convection ovens are good because they swirl the air around inside the oven, creating a mixed mass of warm air without hot or cold spots. Ovens in stoves (if you were tempted) have many cold spots. Make sure that the design of the oven door makes it easy to open the door one-handed and

Convection ovens and toaster ovens are reliable sources of the consistent heat needed for properly curing the polymer clay. Whatever type you choose, use your chosen oven only for polymer clay, never for food, and bake with adequate ventilation, preferably outdoors.

A reliable food processor will assist you in the imitative techniques. A sturdy motor is more important than fancy attachments.

Victoria Hughes, *Geisha Pendant,* 1996. Imitative ivory offers a tempting surface for carving and tinting. The surface painting was done first, then carving to mimic brush-drawn lines, and finally, the filling of those lines with metallic paint.

close it without jarring delicately balanced projects inside.

Convection ovens usually have a larger interior volume. The countertop styles are often a combination of microwave and convection oven. If you are considering purchasing one, make sure you can turn the microwave function off and route all power to the convection function. The microwave will not polymerize the plastic anyway.

Avoid self-cleaning ovens because these spike in temperature from time to time and burn the polymer clay when in the self-cleaning mode.

## buffer or polishing lathe

The polishing lathe is essentially a motor with a shaft extending from either side. The shafts are threaded tapered spindles. Discs of muslin layers are screwed onto the threaded spindles and when the motor is turned on, the rapidly rotating muslin discs polish whatever is pressed up against them.

The terms polishing and buffing are interchangeable for the purposes of this book. I use "buffing" to quickly describe the action, even though the tool is technically called a polishing lathe. I will

often use the word "buffer" to refer to the polishing lathe.

Imitative pieces are polished or buffed as the final post-baking step in bringing up a beautiful luster. I use a Fordham variable-speed polishing lathe, a jeweler's tool. Kathleen Amt introduced me to this particular style lathe. This particular buffer is small, lightweight, and still very powerful and is much more user-friendly for polymer clay than larger grinding wheels and buffers. The compact motor and variable speed allow slower, more controlled polishing.

Polymer clay is a plastic, and all plastics are very temperature-sensitive. Don't use any compound or rouge with the clean muslin discs, as it will fuse onto the polymer clay.

Other tools can be adapted to mimic the buffing action of the polishing lathe. A bench grinder is a larger motor, also with shafts on either end. Bench grinders can be found at most hardware stores and are sold with heavy discs

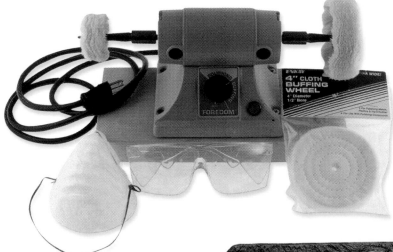

A small polishing lathe will magically transform your pieces from attractive to stunningly beautiful by bringing up a shining gloss on the polymer's surface. Note the safety gear and clean wheel.

Deborah Anderson, *Picture Frame*, 2000. Sensitive attention to subtle colors and patterns re-creates hand-tooled leather in this tender picture frame. The contrast between the polished upper surfaces and the worked background accurately echoes and personalizes true leather.

Photo by Liv Ames.

coated in abrasive grit. These discs can be removed and replaced with muslin discs. Bench grinders are not variable speed but will work for the imitatives. I used one while developing the imitative techniques.

It's also possible to mount an electric screwdriver or drill securely in a vise and use a mandrel of some sort as a shaft in the screwdriver. Attach a muslin disc to this shaft. When the screwdriver is turned on, the muslin disc revolves and polishes.

Muslin discs come in both unstitched and stitched styles. The stitched disc is harder and more aggressive on the polymer: it can remove fine details but is very handy for large smooth areas. The unstitched disc is much softer and good for delicate pieces. I use one of each on my buffer, since there are two spindles.

## horizontal belt sander

A horizontal belt sander is a home woodworking tool. Its motor rotates two horizontal cylinders, around which a continuous 4" by 36" sandpaper belt runs at high speeds. When baked polymer clay is pressed against the moving sandpaper belt, the polymer is sanded away. Because it sands polymer away so enthusiastically, the belt sander creates a lot of polymer dust. Do not breathe this dust (as with any process dust). Always use a dust mask when you sand.

Most brands of these machines have an outlet to attach a vacuum cleaner hose so that you can run the vacuum cleaner as you sand. Set the sander up outside or in a garage where you can open the doors. Consider wearing earplugs.

Coarser-grit sanding belts are available from woodworking supply stores, and are good for the first stages of sanding for shape. These grits do not correspond to the same degree of abrasion as when hand-sanding and, because of the speed, they are more abrasive.

You can find fine-grit sanding belts at plastics supply houses, which stock a specialized type of belt called Trizact. Trizact is not an applied abrasive grit, but rather a surface treatment on the belt itself that creates thousands of fine, precise pyramids that more cleanly sand and smooth the

A belt sander is useful in the imitative techniques, especially for finishing agate. You can make agate without one and be very happy with your work, but if you can try one at some point, do so. Wear a dust mask when you sand with this.

Victoria Hughes, *Ivory Pendant,* 1995. The simplicity of this pendant's silhouette draws attention to its surface details. The delicate image derives from a tear-away transfer of Chinese joss paper done on imitative ivory and antiqued. Leaving the black background matte enhances the lustrous polished ivory surface.

surface of plastics than a random grit. It does not come in different grits but the older and more worn the sanding belt is, the finer the sanding action, as if it was a higher-grit belt. Keep all your old Trizact belts and use them when higher-grit sanding is required. (See page 64 for details.)

## safety equipment

Proper precautions in the studio are vital to your continuance as a happy productive human. Although polymer clay is quite a safe medium–no sparks of hot metal flying around, no molten glass just a foot or two from your arm–there are specific areas of attention.

Be aware of things you breathe and things you get in your body through your skin. Your skin is considered an organ of respiration, like your lungs, and is the largest organ you have. Be careful of your organs!

First, use adequate ventilation for your oven. If you bake in your studio and you go out and come back in, and you can clearly smell baking polymer, you need more ventilation now. Bake outside or in a garage or other uninhabited room. If baking outside, ensure that no direct sun hits the oven, since this throws the thermostat off. Later in the year, be careful that the oven is not too cold and eating up wattage trying to keep itself warm.

Next, always wear a dust mask when sanding and buffing, especially with new muslin discs. As you break in a new disc, you will see a stripe of white powder behind the wheel of the buffer. This is cotton dust. Do not inhale this. Also always wear a dust mask when working with large areas of metallic powder, another material you do not want accumulating in your lungs.

Goggles are for occasions when things may fly up into your eyes.

Wear goggles if you are working with a lot of metallic powders. Wear goggles if you are buffing. Wear goggles if you are cutting a lot of wire and feeling tired. Don't ever mess around with your eyes.

Wear latex or vinyl gloves when using metallic powders or Translucent Liquid Sculpey. Neither of these should be absorbed through your skin. Gloves also prevent embossing fingerprints onto unbaked clay. The fewer fingerprints you get on your piece, the fewer fingerprints you'll have to sand off later.

Two other tools are vital. Bring to your studio a willingness to take chances and the ability to be impressed with yourself for each session of work. These tools are unique to each person and cannot be pictured. But like having a clear glass and a tissue blade, having and using these will dramatically increase the fun and satisfaction you get from your creative process.

Basic safety equipment in the polymer clay studio includes goggles for buffing and when using the belt sander, dust masks for sanding and buffing and when using metallic powders, and latex or vinyl gloves to keep fingerprints off delicate pieces and to protect your skin.

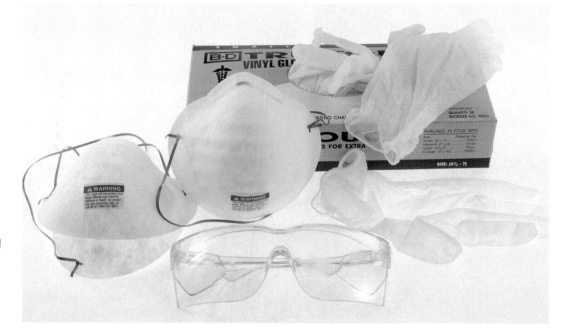

# chapter 4

# foundation processes

## fundamental approaches and techniques
## for working in polymer clay

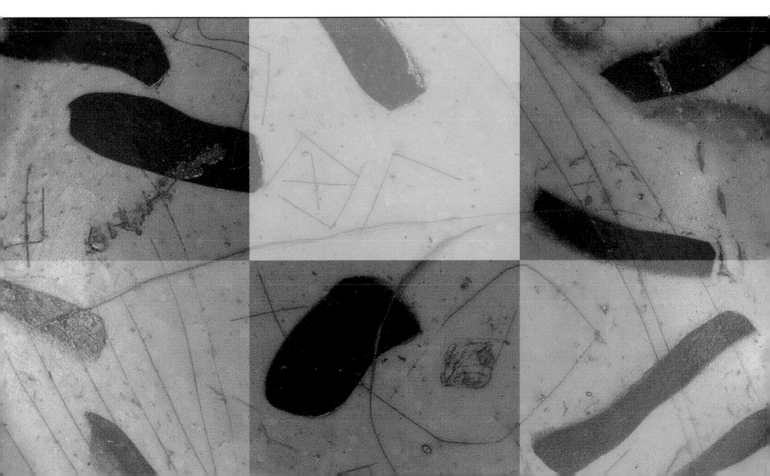

# prebaked processes

## clay body vs. stock

'Clay body' is a term for a mixed ball of clay, not yet made into any form. 'Stock' is a term for unbaked sheets or rolls in specific colors, qualities, and thicknesses that have been prepared or treated in certain ways, but not yet applied to a particular project. Both terms appear throughout the book.

## general guidelines for working with polymer clay bodies

1. Always condition polymer clay. This ensures consistency of the clay body during the making of the piece, and a predictable surface on the piece after baking.

2. Mix your own colors, translucencies, and textures of polymer clay to give yourself a custom palette of materials for your individual creative needs.

3. Familiarize yourself with the different brands and versions of polymer clay. Use each and understand its applicability for your processes.

4. And, of course, *don't burn the polymer*. Baking polymer at too high a temperature is the only real mistake—the only thing you can do wrong to the clay. Everything else, including baking a long time, is fine. Some brands may discolor if baked for a long time, but this is not an error like baking too hot.

The projects in this book are meant to get you started. There's a world of things out there to inspire you to move past the objects shown. Your interests are the compass to follow. These are

Victoria Hughes, *Ivory Tusk Necklace,* 1996. Small glass beads inside this hollow ivory pendant rattle when shook. Molding, carving, wire work, and patinas envelope the tusk in an antique, mysterious feel.

teaching projects, uncomplicated and direct. I have deliberately designed them to emphasize individual aspects of the imitative techniques, like carving, feathering, or translucency. The real delight of these techniques comes from personalizing and combining them, improvising, adjusting, changing subtle things and seeing what happens.

Always follow your internal compass. You'll notice that some of my pieces look more intricate or finished than the projects or the examples. These are one-of-a-kind studio work. Everyone has a learning curve, no matter where they are. The shape of the curve changes, depending on your accomplishments.

## conditioning the clay

You condition clay by folding, twisting, stretching, and refolding until the original packaged texture of the clay is transformed into a smooth, even, homogenous consistency.

*Always condition and mix your colors at the same time.* The amount of physical manipulation required to break down the initial irregularity in unbaked clay is *exactly* the same amount of manipulation required to mix two colors together thoroughly enough to get a third solid color. Unless you are using a color just as it comes out of the package, like white, black, or translucent, condition your colored clays by mixing colors together at the same time to halve the labor, and create your own unique palette of colors.

Begin conditioning by chopping the polymer clay(s) into small pieces. Accumulate an amount that easily fits in your hand.

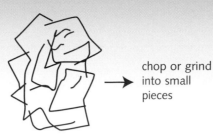

chop or grind into small pieces

Squeeze until this forms a coherent clump. If the clay feels crumbly, add another piece of clay that is more malleable or add Mix-Quick or the translucent version of whatever brand you are using. (If the clay is extremely crumbly and will not consolidate, it may have dried out or may be partially polymerized. In this case, throw the clay away.)

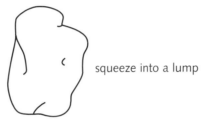

squeeze into a lump

Roll this lump between your palms to form a snake. Fold the snake in half and twist it tightly so it looks like a fat twisted rope.

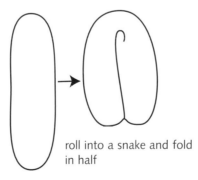

roll into a snake and fold in half

Twist the folded rope.

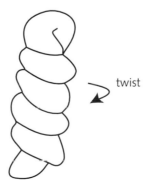

twist

Push this fat twisted rope together across the coils, as if you were closing an accordion. Roll this accordion lump into a snake again.

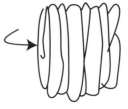

squeeze like an accordion

Repeat this several times— snake, fold, twist, squeeze—until the clay is one solid color, with no streaks or uneven color. When mixing colors, the clays will be properly conditioned when the clay body is a solid color, without striping or marbleizing.

When working with pure black or white, bend the rolled snake in half. Look at the top of the bend. If the clay looks smooth, not striped, and you do not see any variations in surface gloss, the clay is properly conditioned.

There are so many variables that it is impossible to tell you how long conditioning should take. The heat of your hands, the clay's softness, the room temperature, the brand of clay, whether you have small or larger pieces to start with: all contribute to the time necessary.

Translucent polymer clay in all brands tends to be a little softer and more malleable than colored clay of the same brand. To condition translucents properly, manipulate them for as long as you did the colored clays. Translucent clays must be conditioned well or they will not bake as translucent as is possible.

Well-conditioned clay will be evenly smooth on the surface as well as internally. Small bumps and irregularities that appear on the surface after baking are usually signs that the clay was not conditioned well. After the clay is baked and cooled with this bumpy surface texture it is difficult to

Photo courtesy of the artist.

Antoinette Belonogoff, 2001. Attractive colors, molded elements, and surface textures pull together this whimsical pendant.

Victoria Hughes, *Clay Body Book,* 2001. A book of polymer clay bodies. Each page has a different material mixed into the polymer. Sampler books like this are a straightforward way to catalog experiments.

eliminate, so avoid this by conditioning properly.

You can use a food chopper to cut the initial cold pieces of colored raw clay into small, warm nuggets that will be easier to clump, squeeze, and roll. Fimo Classic most often benefits from this. Fimo Soft, Prēmo, and Cernit are easier to work from the beginning and will probably not need this assistance.

Some artists run their polymer clay through the pasta machine to condition it. If this is not done very carefully, air bubbles will be mixed into the clay body, rather than eliminated from the clay body. To prevent this, *always* recondition the clay after using the pasta machine to condition. Roll the clay into a snake, fold, and twist, releasing any small air bubbles that have been compressed into the clay body. If you do use a pasta machine to condition, make sure you feed the clay into the rollers *folded side first*, so any air trapped between clay layers can be squeezed out of the clay by the rollers' action.

## mixing clay bodies

Mixing clay bodies is so much fun! Creating your custom selection of unique clays with a range of colors, translucencies, metallic effects, and different textures is a necessary step to releasing your creative potential. You have control. Enjoy it.

As mentioned in Chapter 3, each brand of clay contributes different characteristics to your clay body. Polymer clays intermix well. Personalize your clay bodies: go ahead and mix the Prēmo with the Fimo Soft, or the Cernit with the Fimo Classic.

On my studio table there are a couple hundred mixed colors, in one- to six-ounce units like "little soldiers," as a student once said. Two-thirds of these are opaque colors, the other third are translucent colors, mostly Fimo Art Translucent, ranging from very pale watery tints to more robust luminous tones. It is possible to have a translucent version of almost every color, as well as an opaque version of every color. The unusual contrast between opaque and translucent clays can be appealing, so I always have both versions of a color available to work with.

I also have metallic Prēmo colors, blended with regular or neon colors to morph them in interesting directions. I have many textured clay bodies with different materials added into them such as spices, embossing powders, different grits and particulates, Mylar confetti, cut-up embroidery floss, and the like. I do many other techniques and projects in addition to the imitative techniques. The assortment of clay bodies on my table supports whatever project I am interested in at the moment.

For the projects in this book, I give you formulas for specific colors and opacities. This is to assist those who like guidance while learning to generate your own color mixes. Follow my guidelines first, then play around. Keep a record of your trials. Experiment with mixing your own clay bodies. This will teach you much more thoroughly than following guidelines.

Start a logbook for yourself. Make copies of the "Good Grid" on page 139 or create your own lab journal from any notebook. Glue baked examples of different colors, opacities, textural effects, metallic effects, and other variations that you accidentally or purposefully create, into this logbook, and then *write down* how you made that sample. I have found my record of experiments invaluable in my work, both as a reference and an inspiration for further technical explorations. Try it.

When mixing colors, mix small bits of the dark color into the lighter color until you reach the desired saturation. If you are not familiar with the density of pigments in the polymer clay, start with small additions. This is especially true when mixing opaque pastels. Always mix small amounts of color into the white clay, never the other way around.

When mixing across brands, as a basic guideline use equal parts of each brand. In special cases, to create a specific color or translucency, you may use an uneven ratio. For instance, if I want a deeply saturated violet translucent clay body, I'll mix a pea-sized piece of Prēmo Violet into an ounce of Fimo Translucent (00), because the Prēmo color is so densely pigmented.

In some imitative techniques, for instance the agate re-creations, one brand of clay is specifically required. All of that technique then should use the same brand, or a mixture of that brand of clay and another that allows the primary clay to dominate. Otherwise the finished pieces will tend to delaminate (one layer peels away from another layer of a different brand).

## understanding opacity and translucency

As mentioned earlier, for almost every color of clay, there is both an opaque version and a translucent version possible through mixing. By expanding your mixed clay body assortment to include both, you've virtually doubled your color choices.

An opaque clay body lets no light through. It is a solid color with no perceivable depth. A completely opaque polymer clay body bounces all the light off its surface right back into your eyeballs. This is true whether the clay is baked or unbaked.

A translucent clay body is one made primarily from translucent clay. The translucent quality will only be fully visible after the clay has baked and cooled. If the baked piece is thin, you will be able to see light through it. If the translucent clay is in layers, there will be visible depth to the layers. Depending on the brand of translucent you used, there may be perceivable pebbling (or there may not). Before baking, translucent clay bodies look waxy: not opaque, not translucent. At this time there are no brands of translucent clay that bake clear like glass.

Imagine a scale running from most opaque clay to most translucent clay. Every clay body you create falls somewhere on this scale, either more opaque or more translucent. This is its degree of translucency or opacity. Refer to this scale while working on the imitative techniques. One of the visual characteristics of any material is its inherent degree of opacity; being able to perceive and re-create this is important to the success of your imitative techniques.

In each brand, the white clay is the most opaque clay. Therefore, the closer a color is to white, the more opaque it is. Think of white as the opacifier for polymer clays. The opacity of the clay, as well as its color, is entirely in your control just by mixing.

Darker and more vivid colors, like purple, red, and magenta are obviously less white than brighter, paler colors. This means the clay body itself is less opaque, more translucent. This translucency dulls the polymer's color after baking. A dark color usually looks duller after being baked, even if it was a bright and perky color when unbaked.

This wheel of tinted translucent clay bodies is all mixed from a proportion of 50 parts translucent clay to two parts colored clay.

## mixing opacities and translucencies

There are several reasons to mix an opaque clay body. The first is to prevent the color shift mentioned above. For this purpose, mix in roughly one part white clay to eight parts of colored clay, creating a clay body whose total volume is 1/10 to 1/8 white. Use this small amount of white in all darker and more vivid colors to keep the clay body opaque and maintain the prebaked tint. If you notice any unwanted color shift in your clays after baking (other than browning caused by an overly hot oven), your clay body is probably translucent enough to need this opacifier.

One reason to mix strongly opaque versions of a color is for their contrast with translucent clays. Another is to supply an opaque background for surface painting techniques. An additional reason is specific to the imitative techniques: some natural materials are completely opaque, so to duplicate them you need a completely opaque clay body. The same is obviously true for translucent natural materials and corresponding clay bodies.

Proportion is the key to mixing translucent-based colors. Translucent clay is essentially raw polymer clay with no pigment or opacifier in it at all. Any amount of color mixed into it will show up after baking, even a film of color that was left on your hands from the last clay you conditioned.

To mix translucent-based clay bodies, the basic ratio is one or two parts colored clay to 50 parts translucent clay. Yes, one or two to 50. Start there. Mix the colors together completely. Bake a nickel-sized test piece of the mixed color. Compare the baked color to the unbaked color. Observe any color shift. Decide whether this is the tint you want.

When satisfied, stick the baked sample on the lump of unbaked polymer clay so you always know what that unbaked clay becomes after baking. You might even bake an extra sample of translucent colors you like and glue it in your logbook.

Some translucent-based colors will be more diffuse than others because of the translucency in the original colored clay. For example, purple in most brands is a more translucent clay than turquoise, and creates a more translucent mixed color. Prēmo's colors are strongly saturated and good for mixing darker, more intense translucencies.

## storing mixed clay bodies

Although polymer clay does not dry out, it is affected by heat, direct sunlight, and airborne dust and contaminants. Store the clays covered and away from heat. I keep mixed colors on my worktable covered with Saran Wrap, which is unaffected by the plasticizer in the clays. Other people keep their clays between sheets of wax paper in plastic storage boxes. If you don't plan to use the clays for several weeks or longer, seal the clays in double plastic bags and store them in the freezer.

Be careful when putting polymer clay in contact with other plastics because the plasticizer may melt the other plastic. Cheaper plastics are most reactive to the plasticizer.

## using a food processor or food chopper

A food processor will chop up large pieces of unbaked polymer clay into smaller nuggets. It will also heat the clay slightly from the friction of the processor's blades pushing through the dense clay. The clay will be chopped and mixed, but will not be blended into a solid color. A food processor handles polymer clay

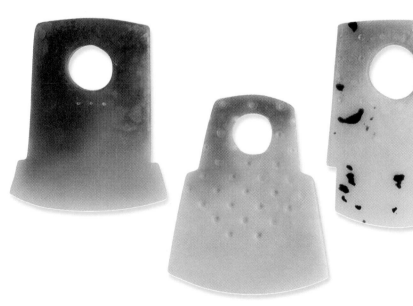

Victoria Hughes, *Jade Pendants*, 2002. Each of these imitative jade pendants incorporated several different translucent-based green clays, illustrating the effectiveness of related translucent colors in mimicking natural materials.

the way it handles hard cheese—it will intermix white and orange cheeses but not create a pale orange cheese product for you.

Never put Cernit in the food chopper, and Prēmo and Fimo Soft only when absolutely necessary. These softer clays get too sticky too quickly and turn into warm blobs that get stuck under the chopper blades, straining the motor. Heat produced by friction on the blades will also begin to polymerize the clay if the motor is left running too long.

Many people use a food processor as an initial stage of conditioning to break the packaged clay into smaller softer pieces that can be more easily manipulated. The food processor can also be viewed as a tool to create small nuggets of unbaked clay. These nuggets can be combined with each other to mimic aggregate materials, or baked as single nuggets, becoming prebaked inlays.

If the clay is too soft to clump easily into the types of shapes you like, chill the polymer and the plastic processor basket and blade in the freezer for 15 minutes, then chop immediately. You may also roll the polymer clay into sheets, layer them between pieces of white paper, and let these layers sit overnight. The extra plasticizer will leach into the paper, leaving the clay stiffer in the morning.

Use a dry paper towel to wipe the smallest clay nuggets from the processor basket, blades, and cover. These small polymer pieces cling from static and should be removed to avoid mixing colors. This is especially important when making nuggets to be baked as is, for pre-baked inlays. If there are random bright-orange spots of clay in your turquoise, it will look wrong.

The plastic processor basket should be cleansed periodically to wash the plasticizer film off. If a film of plasticizer is left on the plastic, it deteriorates the basket, which will craze, get sticky, be harder to clean, and then crack easily. Then you'll have to track down a new basket, which takes time away from your art. It's easier to just clean the basket occasionally instead.

## flattening polymer with a glass

There are two tools that evenly flatten slabs and areas of clay. Each has a specific purpose. Have each tool, and use the right one for the job at hand. One is a straight-sided clear drinking glass and the other is a pasta machine.

The glass can be used with very precise control to flatten to any thinness or thickness, imbed other materials, laminate layers of clay, stretch the surface in specific ways, flatten or smooth clay on a curve, and for many other applications. The pasta machine makes perfectly even sheets in seven to nine precise pasta-oriented thicknesses. It is useful for creating quite long thin sheets of clay, for large sheets, and for sheets whose consistent thickness is imperative.

When flattening anything, first make sure the clay is conditioned properly. Roll a ball of clay between your palms until there are no folds or seams on the ball, then pinch it flat with your fingers to get it closer to the thickness you want.

Use a glass or pasta machine to flatten the slab and smooth the fingerprints. *Please flatten the ball into a slab before you start rolling.* If you make a big ball of clay, then squash a glass down on it and try to roll it flat, the clay will always stick to the glass.

Victoria Hughes, *Postcard,* 1997. Postcards made from Fimo or a Fimo/Cernit mix are sturdy enough to be mailed. After more than a decade of sending them across the globe, I've only lost one. Here, texturing, painting, transfer techniques, carving and prebaked inlays animate the polymer's surface.

Roll with one hand on either side of the glass. Keep the glass parallel to the table unless you are deliberately angling the clay down at the edges. Watch through the glass as you roll over the clay and go slowly. Pay attention to what you are doing, whether flattening or lightly pressing elements into the clay.

Although a clear brayer can be used, its loose handles often add extra uncontrollable play. A solid roller is hard to see through and the narrow rod of plastic distorts your vision of the surface too much to see what effect you are having on the clay.

Gwen Gibson, *Wall Piece*, 1996. Gibson developed the transfer variation called a tear-away, which appears to etch the surface of the polymer. Here, paint was rubbed across the watery lines after baking.

Photo by Robert Diamante.

## flattening polymer with a pasta machine

To flatten slabs of clay with a pasta machine, insert one end of the slab between the rollers and turn the crank. If clay sticks to the rollers, clean them off with premoistened cleansing wipes or alcohol. You may also lay the slab of clay between sheets of baking parchment or wax paper and run this sandwich through the pasta machine. Peel the clay off the paper after it's been flattened out. It's much easier to get the clay off the paper than off the rollers.

Different brands of clay roll differently through the pasta machine. Prēmo flattens out softly and easily. Fimo Soft is similar in consistency but the stiffer Fimo Classic tends to crack open on the edges a bit. Cernit will stick to the rollers often, as will all brands of translucents.

If you give in to the temptation of conditioning clay by running it through a pasta machine, be careful not to trap air bubbles in the clay. Make sure you insert the folded side first so any air trapped between the layers has a chance of being pushed out by the rollers. If the baked pieces frequently have small bumps and eccentricities, check your work habits. These small bumps on otherwise properly baked pieces are air bubbles, trapped in the clay body by your conditioning techniques.

## feathering to blend colors and attach clays

Feathering is a technique that thins one layer of clay over another. It can be a transition between colors, and is also a technique for adding or attaching one piece of polymer to another, baked or unbaked. Imitative jade uses feathering on nearly every piece to merge colors. Most vessels are constructed by attaching different shapes to each other with feathering.

To feather one area of polymer over another, the upper layer must be unbaked but the lower layer can be baked or unbaked. Pinch the front edge of this upper piece into an abrupt wedge, a quick taper. Taper the underlying piece to match, if unbaked.

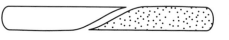

pinch edges of each pad into a crisp abrupt taper

Lay one wedge over the other with the unbaked layer on top. Overlap them so the area of overlap is a little too thick, then pinch this seam area together back to the thickness of the rest of the slab. Fuse the seam between the two pieces of polymer completely by pinching them together.

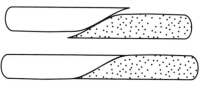

overlap tapered edges and pinch firmly together

Use the broad side of your thumb to brush the edge of the upper clay further out on the lower clay. Drag the clay with the motion of your thumb, thinning it out until there is no clear line between the two colors. This may take some practice. Make sure the original wedge tapers out very thin and that you are using the side of your thumb rather than the tip of your index finger to feather. Stop when the upper color has been blended evenly.

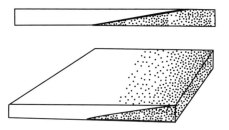

brush gently with thumb and roll to smooth

To add a small section of color to another clay, make a small ball of the colored clay. Pinch the edges of the ball into thin feathered fins and place the feathery ball on the base clay pad. Press the feathered ball firmly into the pad and fuse all the thin edges onto the pad. Feather more by brushing the colored clay out in all directions, using your thumb as above. Roll to smooth.

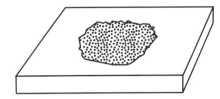

for small elements of blended color

When using this process to attach two baked pieces together, run a small snake of unbaked polymer along the joint—like caulking—and feather each side of the unbaked polymer up onto the baked pieces. Bake. The polymer will securely attach the two elements after baking.

## metallic powders and paints

Although powders and other surface enhancements can be used in all polymer clay techniques, their primary application for imitative techniques is for faux metals. To mimic those you'll use a combination of metallic powders and paints. Wear a dust mask when working with the powders.

Metallic powders will only adhere to the clay before baking. Use your fingers to rub the powders onto the surface. Be sparing with the powders: you can always put more on later, but too much all at once is wasteful and difficult to control. Avoid using a brush as it tends to disperse the powders up into the air.

Make sure the powder is firmly adhered on the surface. Lightly roll across flat pieces of unbaked polymer with a glass to secure the powder on the clay. Remove any excess powder from the surface before baking: it will brush off later, either in the oven or on your work surface.

Designate an area for working with metallic powders, away from your clean work surface. No matter how careful you are, metallic powders blow around and will end up where you least desire them. Wash your hands as soon as you finish working with the powders.

Experiment by using different types of inexpensive eyeshadow as decorative powders. They often appear in pearlescent and metallic tints, are nontoxic, and are fairly stable colors. I also add metallic powders into metallic acrylic paints to enhance the luster of the paint.

Metallic paints work best in combination. I use at least two together at a time, and often mix in additional metallic powder. Any single metallic effect tends to be flat and monochromatic compared to true metals. Smooth painted surfaces will look like worked metal. Paint that is stippled on or given some sort of texture when applied to the polymer, will tend to evoke a cast surface.

Victoria Hughes, *Lidded Jade Bowl,* 1996. Feathering larger sheets of clay together generated the areas of color shading. Small speckled pebbling is inherent in Fimo Translucent; it's the visible structure of polymerized clay, used to good effect in the imitative techniques. The lip on this bowl was attached by feathering from the underside of the joint.

## working with wire, decoratively and functionally

Wire elements can enhance your design and can also serve practical uses, like the eye pins that attach earring findings to the polymer. In both cases, basic wire habits will keep you safe and create the element you want.

To create and attach decorative shapes of wire on the surface of a piece, make posts from the end of the wire to anchor the wire into the polymer. Bend the first 1/8" of wire down at a right angle, make the shape, then bend down the last 1/8". Embed the wire and bake it with the piece. After baking and cooling, gently lift up the wire, put a drop of Zap-a-Gap on each leg, and push it back into its hollow. Let the glue dry.

Wire elements can take unusual shapes and still be functional. For more complex shapes, bend one foot, grip it, then form the wire shape before bending the other

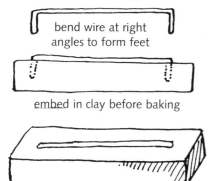

bend wire at right angles to form feet

embed in clay before baking

after baking, lift feet up, glue, reinsert

## note

*Use common sense. Never endanger your own or anyone else's eyes or other body parts. To cut wire, use a good pair of wire cutters. When cut, the pieces of wire are sharp and will fly across the room. Control where the cut piece will go by pointing the end of the wire down onto the table or into your lap before cutting.*

foot. Before embedding, hold the wire shape at eye level to check that the design is all in one plane. In this book you'll see loops for hanging elements, spirals for anchoring loops of wire, coils as tubes that carry necklace cord, and wire eye pins to connect to findings for earrings, and variations on these forms. Experiment on your own with personalizing your wire work.

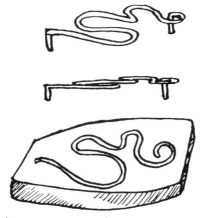

decorative wire work

wire can come off the margin as well as the surface

Coils are best made on a mandrel, which is some type of form around which you can tightly wind the wire. The diameter of the mandrel will be the inside dimension of your coil. If you are using a knitting needle as a mandrel, the thickness of the knitting needle will correspond to the largest thickness of cord that will pass through the coil. As with other techniques mentioned here, practice working with wire and allow yourself a learning curve.

Wrap the wire tightly and evenly on the mandrel, leaving at least 1/2" at each end.

wrap wire around a mandrel

To finish the coil ends and make eye pins, use pliers to grasp the wire, leaving 1/2". With the plier tips tight against the mandrel, twist the pliers back to create an abrupt angle in the wire while maintaining the wire's tightness against the mandrel.

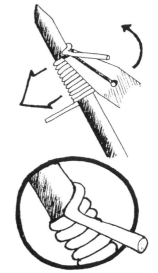

finish coil by bending end

Repeat at the other end of the coil. Be sure both ends of the wire come off the mandrel along the same line.

To check that the ends are correct, sight along the mandrel. The wire ends should be parallel vertically.

It's easiest to make and insert wire elements before baking. With the coil still on the mandrel, insert the wire ends into the clay piece.

repeat at other end

sight along the mandrel to check for alignment

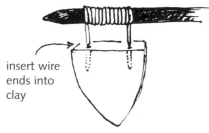

insert wire ends into clay

Press the coil into the holes and carefully remove the mandrel.

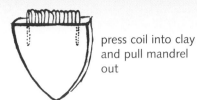

press coil into clay and pull mandrel out

After baking, remove the wire ends, put a drop of glue on the tips, and reinsert them into the clay.

Wire elements can be added to the piece after baking if necessary by drilling a hole the same or a slightly smaller size than the wire, then gluing the wire. Be sure the glue is spread along the wire and goes down into the hole.

Hoops are upside-down u-shaped segments of wire. Hoops create a way to trap a section of wire and hook things together. They need to accommodate the thickness of wire you are using, so make the legs of the hoops long enough to both embed securely in the clay and still protrude high enough to trap that wire.

Spirals can be made tight or loose. To make a spiral for embedding in polymer, first bend an end of wire in a tight right angle, then grip this angled leg with pliers. Wind the wire around itself as you continue gripping the leg. Be slow and deliberate as you pull the wire to keep it even. I wind the wire with my fingers, but you can use a

second pair of pliers to pull the wire into a spiral. For precise loose spirals, wind tight spirals first, then gently open them up.

Eye pins are particularly useful wire elements. Use round-nosed pliers for a smooth shape to the eye. First look at the taper of the pliers. Wrapping wire around the base of the taper, just above the jaw, will give you a big loop of wire. Wrapping around the tip of the pliers will give you a small loop of wire.

Select the loop size you want, and catch the tip of the wire between the corresponding section of the pliers. Hold the free end of the wire in your other hand. Rotate the pliers away from you, curling the tip of the wire back in a half-loop on its shaft, so that it looks like a walking cane. Be sure to rotate the pliers all the way around, so the tip of the wire touches the side of the shaft.

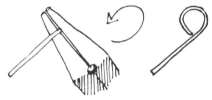

grab wire in pliers and rotate pliers away to form loop

Now you need to center that loop on the shaft. Remove the pliers from the loop. Reinsert the tip of the pliers inside the loop, just above where the loop touches the shaft. Hold tight with your pliers hand.

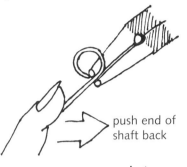

remove pliers and reinsert

With your other hand, push the free end of the wire back, against the pliers, so the shaft moves into alignment under the loop of the wire.

push end of shaft back

The resulting eye pin should look like the illustration.

A further note about eye pins. When opening an eye pin to join it to another loop of wire, be careful to maintain the roundness of the loop. Open the eye by twisting one side of the loop sideways from the shaft. Then close it by just twisting that half back in line with the other side, centered on the shaft. Do not open an eye pin by uncurling the arc of the loop and opening the loop up vertically. This destroys the roundness you worked so hard to get.

finished eye pin

Photo by Liv Ames.

Desiree McCrorey, *Beads*, 2001. Twisted brass wire in the central bead mimics the traditional north African style of mending amber by making a zigzag of wire and running it across splits or fractures in the material.

## embossing

Anything pressed into unbaked polymer will imprint a texture, even such delicate objects as feathers, fingerprints, or fabric. Experiment with this possibility by pressing a piece of conditioned clay against a wide variety of different objects. Bake any that seem interesting and add them to your logbook.

Basic approaches to imprinting pattern and relief include using tools to emboss patterns and shapes, pressing embossing materials against the unbaked polymer to create a pattern or image, and making molds from polymer itself to then use on the clay.

To achieve beautiful imprints on flat clay, make sure the polymer to be imprinted is smooth and free of any texture. If you are embossing with a tool that makes individual marks, like a phillips-head screwdriver or a rubber stamp, emboss the mark, then bake.

To use an embossing plate or other embossing material, or a mold, lay the polymer clay on your work surface, put the embossing material on top of the clay, and roll over both with a glass. If the embossing material or mold is much thicker than the clay, lay the material or mold down first, then put the clay on top. Then either press with your fingers or roll with the glass. To avoid having to peel the embossed clay off the glass, distorting the relief, slip a sheet of paper between the clay and the glass. If necessary, peel the clay off the paper.

To emboss a pattern around the curved surface of a bead, make a smooth ball of clay and carefully pierce a hole through it. Insert the fattest knitting needle you have, and use that as a handle to roll the unbaked clay firmly against your embossing material. If the needle sticks to the inside of the polymer tube, coat it with a release agent like cornstarch before inserting it in the tube. Bake the bead on the knitting needle by suspending it on a tray on two pieces of scrap clay. Or slip the bead off the needle and stand it on end on a tray to bake.

## using a release agent or mold release

To keep polymer clay from sticking to an embossing material or mold, coat the clay with cornstarch or another type of mold release. *Release agent* or *mold release* refers to any substance that accomplishes this. This is vital in working with molds and embossing materials of any kind. Release agents can be powders or films. Wear a dust mask when using airborne particulates like release agents.

Cornstarch is the most common and nonhazardous release agent. Others are dry pigments like oxide, fine dirt, clay, or ash. For decorative effects, use powdered pigment, metallic or iridescent powder, and inexpensive

Antoinette Belonogoff, *Molded Elements*, 2001. A quartet of molded pieces painted differently. Try unexpected colors, translucencies, and amounts of paint on the surface of your pieces. Playfully experimenting with the painting can personalize and animate your work, giving it a distinctive style of your own.

Photo courtesy of the artist.

Photo by Don Felton.

eyeshadow. Avoid talcum powder, which is unhealthy when inhaled. If using a cornstarch baby powder, get one that has no perfumes or moisturizers, which leave a visible residue on the clay.

To use a mold release, thoroughly coat the front and back of the unbaked clay with the release agent. Don't be stingy, cornstarch is cheap. Always put the release agent on the clay, not on the mold or embossing material. Putting the release on the mold fills the finer details with cornstarch, and they will not emboss crisply into the polymer clay.

If an embossing material has a delicate, absorbent surface (like fine unglazed porcelain) or if it has some kind of finish on it (like a lacquer), it requires a release agent. Without one, plasticizer will leach into the embossing material, staining and potentially deteriorating the surface.

For high-relief molds and textures (like pieces of coral or any deeply jagged surface), glycerin works well as a release agent. Rub on a few drops evenly around the unbaked clay, leaving a film on the surface. As the clay stretches to accommodate the drastically increased surface area of a high-relief mold, the glycerin film stretches with the clay, continuing to protect the clay surface from sticking.

Embossed patterns are more visible if some kind of color is applied to the surface, either as a powder before baking or as a paint after baking. Embossing is also more visible when done on light-colored clays, where the shadows of the texture can be easily perceived. Embossed pieces can be

Dayle Doroshow, *Imitative Ivory Face Beads,* 2000. A collection of molded, modeled, painted, and antiqued ivory beads.

baked and finished as is; or used as prebaked elements to be added to other pieces and baked again. I have a large collection of baked, embossed, painted pieces, ready to be inlaid or added to other pieces. These are inspiring to have around for quick assemblage pieces.

# making and using molds

Many of the imitative techniques use molds to develop forms and generate surface and dimensional relief. Good mold techniques will serve you well and assist you in making and using your own one-of-a-kind molds to imprint the clay.

There are several different types of molds. Some are flat pads with surface textures or patterns, some are shaped receptacles like gelatin molds. Molds can also be rollers covered with embossed patterns or textures that lay down continuous swaths of that pattern.

To make flat pad molds or embossing surfaces, always begin with a smooth and well-conditioned pad of polymer clay. For molds made by carving into baked clay, make pads that are smooth on both sides. This will give you twice as many surfaces to use. You can even use the edges to carve narrow bands of patterns for embossing.

To make molds of pre-existing surfaces, make pads of clay that are at least two or three times as thick as the depth of the relief you are copying (minimum 1/4" thick). Use scrap clay that you've mixed evenly into a solid color. Coat this smooth, unbaked pad of clay front and back with cornstarch. *Firmly* press or roll the clay over the relief. Carefully transfer the clay pad to the oven and bake.

When making your own molds, be sure to bake them for at least three hours at 275°F. This baking time may be accumulated over several days, or done all at once. Molds receive a lot of physical pressure on their finely detailed surfaces. To make and maintain as sturdy a mold as possible, bake it a long time to properly polymerize the clay.

To carve your own embossing surfaces or molds, make smooth pads as outlined above and bake

them free of all texture. Everything on a mold will show up. After baking, either carve a freehand pattern or image, draw an image on the surface and carve that, or transfer a pattern or image and carve that away. (See the carving section on page 65 for more about carving techniques.)

Making a classic cup-shaped mold is simple with polymer clay. The shape of the object you are molding is most important—there must be no undercuts on the object. Any object that was originally made from a mold will be fine. Think bowl as opposed to vase.

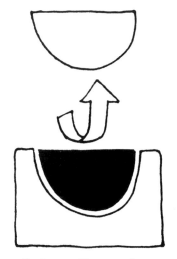

smooth shape with no undercuts easily lifts out of mold

undercuts distort object when it's lifted out of mold

To create a press mold, make a pad of clay at least two to three times as thick as the relief to be molded. Again, at a minimum the clay should be 1/4" thick. The larger the diameter of the mold, the thicker the clay should be to prevent flexing. Liberally apply a release agent to the clay. Press the object firmly into the clay, holding it down with one hand while pushing the edges of the clay up against the object with the other hand. This ensures a precise mold with edges that are as well defined as its center. Avoid accidentally repositioning the object in the clay as you press, as this will blur the detail. Bake.

molding object with no undercuts →

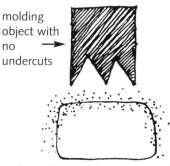

well-conditioned clay at least twice as thick as molding object, liberally coated with release agent

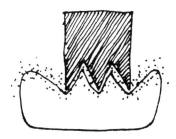

push molding object firmly into the clay – no wiggling or it will smear the impression

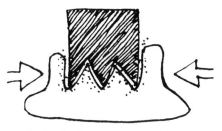

push clay back in against molding object to finish edge detail

To create a roller mold, pierce a hole through the exact center of a plug of polymer. If the hole is not centered, you will have to roll more lightly on one side than the other to compensate for the irregular width of the tube. Put the clay tube on a thick knitting needle and texture it on the needle. Then bake the roller mold by suspending the bead and knitting needle on two piers of scrap clay so the mold's surface does not flatten out on contact with the baking tray.

You can also work back into the unbaked clay of the mold. For example, in making a mold from a button, you might press the tip of a knitting needle in a pattern around the edge of the unbaked button shape. These rounded pits will appear as a pattern of raised bumps on the positive.

Polymer clay is extremely sensitive to textures. A mold should contain as much detail as the original. If your mold detail is not as crisp or precise as you'd like, press harder and use more mold release. Instinctively you will not push hard against something you are afraid may get stuck. Pay attention to what you are doing and work deliberately. Don't rock your fingers on the clay while pressing.

## baking and rebaking

When doing basic baking, accurately preheat the oven to 275°F and bake the clay at least 20 to 30 minutes. Depending on the type of clay and the specific technique, baking time may vary but never the baking temperature. When in doubt, read the manufacturer's directions on the package.

Get a separate oven that you will only use for polymer clay and set it up outside or in the garage or on a patio. Do not put it in the direct sunlight or in a strong cold wind.

To test for proper baking, bake a nickel-sized test piece, ideally Fimo Art Translucent, and let it cool to room temperature. Press your fingernail into an inconspicuous edge. The clay should dent but not chip. If the clay chips easily, or breaks when you bend your test piece, either the temperature is too low, or you did not bake the piece long enough. After baking, Fimo Art Translucent will be waxy, not milky looking, with small pebbling or plaquing.

Baking is the only polymer clay process where it is possible to make a real mistake. Above 300°F all polymer clays are *too hot*. First they get brownish, then they become shiny, then the browning increases and the shininess turns to a bumpy, blistered surface, then the browning turns to blackening, and the surface bursts into flames. At this point the clay emits clouds of hazardous smoke. Sounds terrible, right? Right! *Never* burn polymer clay. Profit from my personal experience. Make sure the oven temperature is accurate and that no paper armature elements touch the heating elements and catch on fire. Get a separate thermometer if you're not sure, and always do test samples first.

Baking time can vary depending on the type of clay. The longer a piece bakes, the more durable the polymer itself becomes. This is true of all types of clay baking at any temperature below 300°F. Both Fimo Classic and Soft will tolerate hours of baking, making them good candidates for multiple baking techniques. This is true even of Fimo white. Cernit cannot be baked more than 30 minutes or so without starting to discolor. Prēmo white, as well as all brands of translucent and translucent colors, will brown after 40 minutes or so, although darker colors will not show much change. Liquid Sculpey, or TLS, will gradually brown over longer baking times. These color shifts are an indicator of baking time and they are inevitable. To avoid them, either bake these pieces only once or plan the construction of your pieces to add these areas in the last baking.

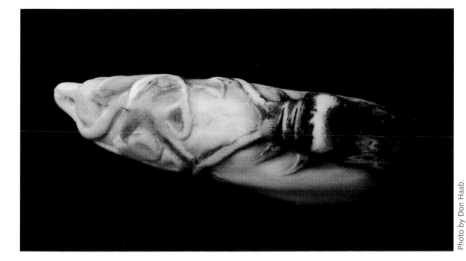

Photo by Don Haab.

Jacqueline Lee, *Beetle Netsuke*, 2001, This sensitive re-creation of an antique ivory netsuke was molded in a translucent ivory polymer, baked, then tinted carefully with oil paints.

TLS ideally bakes at 300°F for 10 minutes. It is most translucent when baked under these conditions. It also becomes incredibly durable and flexible (a thin piece can be tied in a knot without ill effects). When necessary, TLS can be baked with regular polymer clay at 275°F for 30 minutes: the Liquid Sculpey will be polymerized but will not become as translucent or as durable as when baked at a higher temperature. When baked this long, it will tend to yellow a bit.

All polymer clays soften slightly while baking before they polymerize and become rigid. Some thin-walled and open shapes need an armature or support to maintain their shape during baking. I use curled or pleated paper for most of this temporary bracing, or suspend the piece during baking if the shape permits. Polyester batting is a useful support for odd polymer clay shapes. The batting conforms to the unusual shapes and the polymer is suspended while hardening, avoiding the creation of a flat spot.

Polymer clay will take an impression of whatever it is baked against. Baking right on the tray of the oven will emboss a flat spot on the piece and, if you are making flat pieces, this is not a problem. Glass will give polymer a smooth surface. Paper will emboss its texture on the clay. Use paper without photocopy or ballpoint pen images, as these will transfer onto the clay.

## prebaked inlays

Thin sheets and other shapes of polymer clay, in different colors, textures, and effects, can be baked when it is convenient and used when the desire arises. After the sheet is baked you may cut it into smaller pieces with scissors or an X-acto knife, then set the prebaked elements in unbaked clay and bake again.

thin baked element

When pressing the prebaked piece into unbaked clay, press the inlay almost flush with the surface, allowing it to protrude above the surface just a bit. Pressing the inlay into unbaked clay creates a gap between the baked and unbaked clay. You can leave this gap and bake as is, then fill it with paint after baking to accentuate the inlay, or you can press the unbaked clay back against the inlay before baking. If you apply paint to the gap, do it after sanding and before buffing.

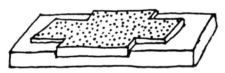

press inlay firmly into unbaked clay

When you sand the final project, you will sand the inlays flush with the surface, which gives them a lovely authentic feel.

Prebaked inlays must be baked a standard 30 minutes. If the clay is underbaked, the thin pieces will chip when you try to cut them into precise shapes. If the inlay is made from a type of clay that will discolor with additional baking time, make and cut the prebaked inlay and press it into the appropriate place in the piece to mold a resting place for it. Before baking, remove the inlay, bake the piece, then glue the inlay back in place with Zap-a-Gap.

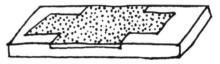

baked together and sanded flush after baking

You may also bake canes, tubes, and any other shape or surface to inlay. Imitative techniques are good inlays—the finishing may be done at the same time as the underlying project, or you can finish the prebaked sheet itself and avoid that step once you've cut the tiny shape out. I have also used prebaked inlays with molded surfaces, as well as photocopy transfers and painted effects.

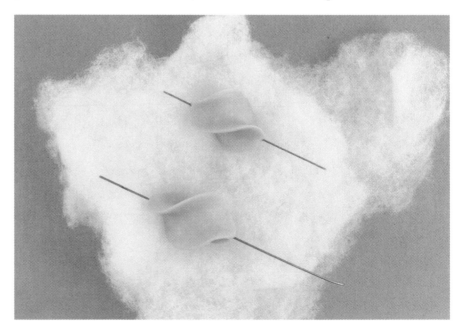

Organically shaped jade beads being baked on a nest of polyester batting to maintain their shape during the softening stage of polymerization. The beads are still on the wires on which they were formed to prevent distorting the shape when the wires are removed.

## prebaked checkerboard canes for inlays

Checkerboard canes are simple to construct and are useful for inlays. I construct the cane, then cut it into several sections and reduce each a different amount. Then I bake the canes, slicing off pieces as I need them rather than baking individual slices.

Polymer clay is ideally suited to caning or millefiore. Many books about polymer clay techniques go into more detail than I have room for here. See pages 143-144 for a list of suggestions. This simple cane can get you started, though.

Begin with well-conditioned 2" square by 1/4" thick clays pads, rolled smooth.

1/4" pads

Lay one square on top of the other and gently compress the two pieces.

gently compress

Cut in half precisely. The resulting pieces should be 1/2" high, 1" wide, and 2" long.

cut in half precisely

Lay one cut half on top of the other. This piece should measure 1" high, 1" wide, and 2" long.

lay one half on top of other

Slice the combined piece as wide as the layers are high. The slices should be about 1/4" wide.

slice

Flip over every other slice.

flip over alternate slices

Compress to consolidate the slices into one block.

consolidate

If desired, you can reduce the size by gently stretching out the cane.

gently stretch out the cane

Bake as a solid cane, then slice after baking.

Victoria Hughes, *Inlaid Ivory Key Necklace,* 2001. This strung collection of inlaid ivory beads emphasizes color and evocation in its prebaked elements. Some of the additional patterning was done before baking, by embossing, and the remainder was carved and antiqued after baking. Individually chosen, nonrepeating beads between the ivory pieces sustain the sense of personal design.

# postbaked processes

**DO THESE TECHNIQUES IN THIS ORDER**

MANTRA

SAND
CARVE
PAINT
BUFF

## hand sanding

Sanding is the necessary first step for finishing almost all imitative techniques. *Always sand under water*, using wet-or-dry sandpaper. Rinse the sandpaper frequently. Water keeps the polymer dust from clogging up the grit of the sandpaper and from rising up into your lungs. Dry-sanding polymer will not work well.

Sandpaper needs to be used in order of grit size, starting with the most abrasive and moving to finer grits. The higher the number of the grit, the finer it is. For the purposes of this book, think of wet-or-dry sandpaper starting at 120-grit (the most abrasive) and becoming increasingly fine up to 1500-grit (the finest). Higher grits are available but difficult to find. The baked smoothness of polymer clay is equivalent to about a 400-grit, so think of that as the midpoint. Grit sizes lower than 400-grit (120, 220, 320) abrade away the baked clay. Grit sizes above 400-grit smooth the clay, and the finer the grit the more light the refinement of the surface.

Each increasingly higher grit size leaves finer and shallower scratches on the surface of the clay. If you go directly from a very coarse grit to a very fine grit, you will have only smoothed off the upper peaks of the deep scratches left by the coarse grit.

To refine the contours of a piece after baking, start with 220-, then 320-grit wet-or-dry sandpaper. The papers should be wet before using, and may be soaked for up to a week to keep the backing material supple while you are using it.

To smooth pieces that are the desired shape and prepare them for polishing, use 400-, then 600-, then 800-, 900-, or 1000-grit. For very high shine, sand with a 1500-grit also. The higher the grit used for sanding, the higher the gloss after buffing, and the quicker that gloss is achieved.

To create a surface for painting, sand with at least 600-grit. The act of baking polymer clay develops the effect of a glazed or fused layer on the outer surface. It is not a true glaze, as on a ceramic, but an impervious surface that sheds water, and to which paint will not easily adhere. This surface layer must be removed if you are planning to paint or buff your finished piece.

MORE ABRASIVE                                    SMOOTHER

120  220  320-Grit        **400**-Grit    600   800-    1000-    1500-Grit
                                                    900     1200

equivalent to a baked
polymer surface
wherever you start and stop on this scale, use each grit in order going up – 320, 400, 600 not 320, 600

Often a baked surface has micro-irregularities, invisible before you polish the piece, but highlighted by the buffing. Sanding away the top layer removes these irregularities. It also gives a more absorbent, open surface to the clay.

## texturing: scribing, scratching, marking, cutting

To texture means to mark baked polymer clay by scribing, scratching, cutting, drilling, carving, and other physical actions. Baked polymer is easy to work back into, using either manual or power tools.

To scribe, incise lines into the surface of the baked clay with a needle tool in a controlled manner. Scratching is more random, unpredictable mark-making and can be done with anything abrasive enough to bite into the baked polymer surface, such as needle tools, coarse sandpaper, files, sharp stones, and the like.

To cut, use a knife, scissors, or a tissue blade to affect the shape of a baked edge. Thick polymer can be cut with an X-acto knife or tissue blade. Scissors will easily cut through thin clay. For example, you can cut a notch out of the upper margin of a pendant with an X-acto knife or use decorative scissors to shape the edge of a thin sheet of polymer. Prebaked sheets used for inlays can be cut with scissors or even a decorative punch if the clay is well-baked and thin enough.

## carving

To carve away lines in a design, use a linoleum cutter or other carving tool. The gestures are identical to those used in carving printing blocks from wood or

Photo by Kojo Kamau.

Debora Jackson, *African Neckpiece and Earrings,* 2000. Striking carving energizes this dramatic necklace and earring set. Confident and careful, the line-carving over the ivory evokes the personality of its creator and cultural associations.

Victoria Hughes, *Tawny Bowl,* 1992. After baking and sanding, I scratched patterns into the surface of this bowl with a needle tool, then rubbed red oxide paint into the marks. The small pits arose from fine grit that was mixed into the clay body. When the bowl was sanded, some of the grit fell out, leaving pits to the paint.

linoleum. Carve into the piece itself, leaving an incised line, or carve onto a baked polymer pad, then emboss that carved pattern on your piece, leaving a raised line. This embossing plate can be used in combination with carving on the piece for exceptional textural richness.

To carve away dimensional areas, use an X-acto blade to cut straight down into the clay, then slide the blade sideways across the cut and lift the isolated polymer away. Continue by filing and sanding to refine the forms.

Please adhere to the following basic safety rules, which are all aimed at controlling the blade. Always press the piece onto the table, holding it down with one hand, and carve with the other hand. Never carve holding the piece up in the air and scratching at it with the carving tool. In addition to being dangerous, this is ineffective. Never aim the tool toward your holding hand. As always, protect your hands.

As with all sharpened tools, keep carving blades in good condition. When a tool gets dull, you will tend to instinctively push harder. This lessens your control over the tool, making it more likely that the blade will slip. After time, these blades may get little nicks and chips. At this point, just wiggle the blade out of the handle and glue in a new one.

To carve, begin with a well-conditioned and well-baked pad of clay. Use both hands to carve. Hold the piece to be carved firmly down on the table with your non-carving hand. You'll also use this hand to rotate the piece under the blade. Hold the carving tool easily in your carving hand.

When carving, practice really does make perfect. Don't be impatient, just practice.

Your carving hand will push the blade through the clay and thus determine the speed, and to

some extent, the direction of the cut. This hand also controls the depth of the cut. To maintain control over the cut, giving you precisely what you want, your carving hand must never be at an awkward angle. Especially when practicing, keep checking that your position is easy. Do you feel relaxed and in control of the carving? Watch your hands. Do they look comfortable? If not, adjust your position.

Use your noncarving hand to keep the piece firmly pressed against the work surface. Move the piece under the blade, rotating the piece into the path of the blade. Avoid using your carving hand to push the blade across the stationary piece, because you'll end up with your hand at a very awkward angle to your wrist, with no control at all, heading into your chest. Eeek. Go slowly and use control.

Vary the pressure of the blade on the clay. Pressing harder makes a deeper cut and a wider line. A soft, shallow cut creates a finer line. Don't push the blade lower into the clay than the depth of the blade. Try it: you'll see that this rips up the edges of the cut, giving an uncontrolled ragged edge to your line.

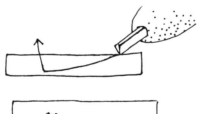

never cut deeper than the blade or you will have a ragged edge on the cut

Experiment with different shaped blades too. A v-shaped blade creates a different cut than a u-shaped blade.

Experiment with the end of the cuts. For a straight, perpendicular

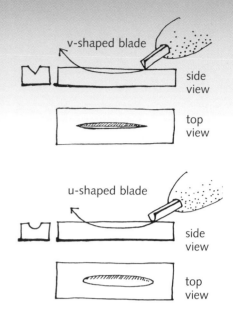

v-shaped blade — side view — top view

u-shaped blade — side view — top view

end to the cut, flick the blade up cleanly where you want to terminate the line. The end of the cut will be relatively abrupt and clean.

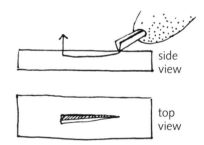

straight perpendicular end to the cut

Gently swing the blade up as you finish off the cut and you'll see that the line ends in a taper, as it began.

For right-angled cuts, butt one straight end against the side of another.

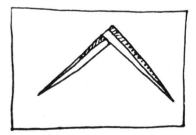

cuts at right angle

For calligraphic, thick, and thin lines, vary the pressure.

Remember that the depth of the cut equals the width of the line. If you gently turn the piece while carving, you can achieve the both thick and thin cuts.

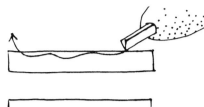

OR

calligraphic lines

## drilling

Baked polymer clay is soft enough to be drilled by hand. Hand drilling is much more controllable than an electric drill. As suggested in the materials and tools section, buy a range of drill bits and bake them in polymer clay handles that fit your hand.

Drilling is straightforward. To drill holes for wire attachments use a bit the same size or, if necessary, slightly smaller than the wire. With most baked polymer clay pieces, the snug fit of a thicker wire means a more secure joint. However, on a thin piece of clay there will be a visible bulge on the outside of the piece if the wire is larger than the hole. This is most likely to happen with earrings, when a hole has been drilled for an eye pin into the top margin and the wire is too heavy a gauge.

Drilling can be used to connect elements that may not have enough contact area for a stable glued joint. If two baked pieces touch at a point, drill 1/4" into each piece at the contact point. The holes must line up perfectly.

Then slip a 1/2" piece of inflexible spring steel wire into one hole and slide the other hole over it. Use Zap-a-Gap on the ends of the wire. The pin of steel wire will securely join the two elements at that point.

If you are doing a lot of production work, consider purchasing a drill press to quickly and accurately drill similar objects. There are small tabletop styles available.

## paints for antiquing, coloring, and metallicizing the surface

*Acrylic paint stains clothes if not immediately washed out of the fabric.* Wear an apron or old shirt when working with paints. Most painting in these techniques is done using fingers rather than brushes, so the paint gets around.

Acrylic paints are a type of polymer and are very compatible with polymer clay. For the purposes of this book, acrylic paints are used as surface paints, to antique the clay, to mimic metals, and to tint or color carved areas. Acrylic paints are also used as a

Victoria Hughes, *Octopus*, 1997. Dimensional carving in polymer. I began by covering an egg-sized rock with 1/2" thick ivory polymer clay stock then baked it, leaving the rock inside for heft. I line carved the octopus into the clay first, defining the forms; then worked the forms in dimensionally with an X-acto knife. I smoothed the contours with files and sandpaper. The motif continues underneath, with corals and seaweed on which the octopus is perched. One of a series emulating Japanese netsuke, examining the natural world.

thin layer of polymer inside the agate clay body.

In general in the imitative techniques, acrylics are used without dilution. It is easier to control the paint if it is not too runny. For antiquing, keep a damp paper towel handy to moderate the wet paint on the surface of the baked piece and work until the nuances of tint satisfy you.

When polymer clay bakes, a fused layer sets up on the surface, like the glaze on ceramics. This layer has a water-resistant surface and does not hold paint. Paint applied to an unsanded polymer surface will wipe off easily and subtle control of the paint will be almost impossible. Sanding removes this layer, exposing a more absorbent surface like tooth on a piece of watercolor paper. You may notice where you've sanded unevenly by the areas on a painted piece that are the original clay color.

When the paint on a piece is right, you can put it back in the oven for 10 minutes. Heat sets polymers. This short rebaking cures the paint on the surface of the polymer clay, permanently adhering it. The same thing will happen over time if you wait a few days for the paint to cure at room temperature. Polishing after setting the paint ensures that the buffer is less likely to remove that thin upper layer of paint.

Once you set the paint like this, the only way to remove paint from the surface is by sanding. Sanding will remove delicate nuances of paint and creates a sharp distinction between dark paint and light polymer. Make sure the paint suits you before you set it. Sanding later is possible and looks fine but it gives a different feel to the surface.

## buffing or polishing

Re-creating the gloss of an antique, much-handled object is one of the main objectives of the imitative techniques. This sheen arises from sanding the surface well, and then polishing.

If you plan to do much polishing, purchase a polishing lathe or buffing wheel. A bench grinder can be converted into a buffer by replacing the grinding wheel with a muslin disc. If you don't have access to a polishing or buffing tool, sand your pieces with the finest sandpaper available, and polish them briskly with a soft rag. You can also lightly apply neutral shoe polish to the surface, then polish with a clean soft rag.

!BUFFING
• PULL LONG HAIR BACK
• REMOVE NECKLACES
• PUT ON DUST MASK
• AND GOGGLES
SAFETY!

### note

*Proper safety precautions are vital when polishing. Follow the instructions that come with the machine. Use a dust mask to avoid inhalation of the muslin dust, especially with new wheels. Breathing cotton dust is bad for you. Make sure you are not wearing any clothing or jewelry that might get tangled up with the shaft as you stand over it. Tie your hair back. Wear goggles to protect your eyes from pieces that may fly off the sander. Always take care of your body, it's the only vehicle you get.*

The buffing wheel is a motor with a shaft on either end, each of which is threaded to accept polishing discs. I keep an unstitched muslin disc on one side and a wider stitched disc on the other. Never use any compound or polishing rouge on the discs: polymer clay is so heat-sensitive that the friction of polishing will fuse any compounds onto the surface of your piece.

The lathe in the illustration has a variable speed motor to allow slow and gentle polishing on delicate shapes and moderately fast polishing for basic buffing. High speed buffing removes the surface and should only be done deliberately and occasionally. Remember, the buffing wheel spins *toward* you, very fast.

### Buffing Basics

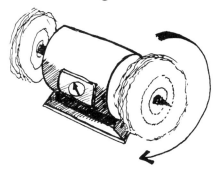

1. Hold piece in lower front quarter of wheel. Never reach past axle or midpoint.

2. Keep piece moving against wheel. Do not let it rest in one place.

3. Use both hands to hold and control piece.

4. Never grab where you just polished.

5. Be prepared. The wheel will snatch and fling pieces away from you.

To polish, turn the buffer on. Use a midrange speed if you have this option. Notice that the wheels (the muslin discs) spin toward you. Hold your piece in the lower front quadrant of the wheel. Here you have maximum control over your piece.

Hold your piece securely. If it is a bead, jam it tightly on a knitting needle, which then can be used for a handle. If it is a flat object, hold the edges with one hand and keep the other hand underneath, supporting the object as you gently press it up against the wheel.

Keep your piece constantly in motion, moving it in small circles against the disc. Move it forward and backward, so you are pressing a little harder sometimes, a little more gently at other times. If the polymer stays in one position too long, the friction of the moving wheel will heat and soften the clay; small fibers from the wheel will fuse to the softened clay, and long grooves will be worn into the polymer.

Never put your fingers where you just buffed. When the polymer is still warm from being polished, it will take an impression of whatever is pressed tightly against it, like your fingerprints. Fingerprints that happened after polishing require you to resand, repaint, and repolish. It's best to develop good polishing habits now and avoid holding your piece while it's warm.

To see polishing techniques in action and increase your understanding of what polishing lathes do and how best to work with them, see any of my videos on the imitative techniques, listed on page 143.

## gluing polymer and mixed media

Polymer clay's low baking temperature allows you to assemble and bake all the elements of your design at the same time. Some materials, primarily other plastics, will fuse to the clay during baking. Each element you bake with the polymer leaves a matching indentation into which it fits. Lift each nonfused element up after baking, put a drop of the appropriate glue in that indentation, and press the object firmly back down.

Use Sobo for porous materials, before or after baking. Use it also as an intermediate layer to tack things together during baking, like a fusible interfacing layer in fabric construction. Sobo can be applied to either the clay or the material to be adhered. Spread a thin layer on the clay or material. Always let the glue dry. When wet, white glue acts like a lubricating layer, rather than an adhesive.

Sobo is also used as a thin protective coating over porous materials that you may want to lacquer later. Lacquer often saturates paper and fabric, giving it a wet look and occasionally smearing the printing inks. The dried glue prevents the lacquer from saturating the paper. Coat the paper or fabric piece first with Sobo, let it dry, then incorporate the glued piece into your design and bake it.

Use Zap-a-Gap for nonporous materials, after baking and cooling. Excessive heat makes the glue more brittle and not as adherent. Do not reposition or wiggle the elements when working with Zap-a-Gap. The glue's first contact with the polymer is its only secure bond. Slo-Zap is slightly more forgiving; you have one or two seconds to reposition the elements.

Glass and other nonporous materials have smooth, slick surfaces that are difficult for the glue to adhere to. Rough up the contact area of these materials by using 80-grit sandpaper or a file to abrade their surfaces.

Keep caps securely on the bottle. When uncured, these glues begin to deteriorate as soon as they contact air. Over time, the unused glue in an open bottle becomes less sticky and more gelatinous. Buy a new bottle of glue at this point. There are two dropper tips available: use those, not an intermediate tool to transfer Zap-a-Gap to your piece.

Avoid using too much glue: it diminishes the stickiness of this type of glue and will leave a raised shiny spot. The only way to remove excess dried glue is to sand it off, which then necessitates repainting and repolishing. Be attentive when using these glues.

Zap-a-Gap, like all cyanoacrylate glues, really will bond your skin together along with anything else nearby. Once I glued my fingertips together while attaching a post back to an earring. The post back was between my fingertips, glued in there too. The only recourse is to soak the glued areas in nail polish remover, which softens the glue and allows you to pull things apart slowly.

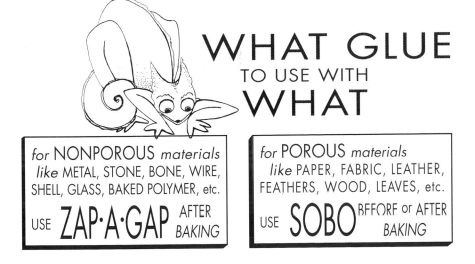

# WHAT GLUE
## TO USE WITH
# WHAT

for NONPOROUS materials like METAL, STONE, BONE, WIRE, SHELL, GLASS, BAKED POLYMER, etc.
USE ZAP·A·GAP AFTER BAKING

for POROUS materials like PAPER, FABRIC, LEATHER, FEATHERS, WOOD, LEAVES, etc.
USE SOBO BEFORE or AFTER BAKING

## lacquering polymer clay

In general, imitative techniques should not be lacquered. There are only three occasions when lacquering these pieces is appropriate.

1. To shine up areas that are difficult to polish, but that would be polished in the original, such as the inside of a polished bowl.

2. To give a high and permanent gloss to selectively chosen areas of an object, especially on an object that itself will not be polished. An example of this is shining up small lapis inlays in a sandstone bowl.

3. To protect vulnerable surface techniques such as delicate paintings from being abraded or rubbed away.

Apply lacquers in a dry environment and in a well-ventilated room to avoid inhalation of the fumes. Always read the manufacturer's instructions.

Golden brand polymer varnishes should be diluted with water and applied slowly to prevent small air bubbles from being trapped in the drying varnish. Golden matte varnish can be buffed to bring up highlights on raised areas. This lacquer also is

UV-protectant. This is my varnish of choice for the imitative techniques.

Apply Fimo lacquer evenly and without hesitation, as it dries quickly and any small retouching leaves visible marks. If this happens, reheat it in the oven for 10 minutes to soften the lacquer slightly. This smooths out some of the more egregious bumps and streaks. As with most coatings, two thin coats are better than one thick coat. This lacquer tends to be brittle, so it is best on pieces that will not flex and crack the varnish.

Jean Cohen, *Ivory Inlaid Pendant,* 2000. Embossing of various textures, prebaked inlays, line carving, and the addition of beading around the edge of this piece add whimsy to the underlying personalized approach to ivory.

# having
# fun

When I look back over 30 years of working with this material, 20 of them professionally, my own enjoyment and delight has been the ticket to my satisfaction and the success of my work. After selling my work at upper-end shows for 10 years, I am convinced that people are as aware of the presence the artist brought to making the piece as they are to the concept or colors the artist chose.

In other words, if I love what I am doing when I make something, then that joy is in the piece. Most people feel that, and they want to share in it. Many of you have experienced having someone want to buy a piece you made for yourself, for fun, where you really played around with the design and materials. So go for it. Embrace this delight fully. You are here to enjoy yourself, you know.

Although sometimes the days are long and other aspects of life try to convince you that they are the only reality, this is not true. The truth is that whatever you are doing and feeling and thinking in this moment is real for you. Have a good time with it. Return to that fun-filled exploration you learned as a kid. It's still inside of you. Polymer is the perfect medium for this, have you noticed?

When you are having fun, enjoying what you are doing, not only do you feel good, which is good for your health, but you accomplish your desires, and you add joy to the overall mood of people around you. Happiness radiates outward, like ripples of light in a pond.

Victoria Hughes, *Armillary,* 1993.

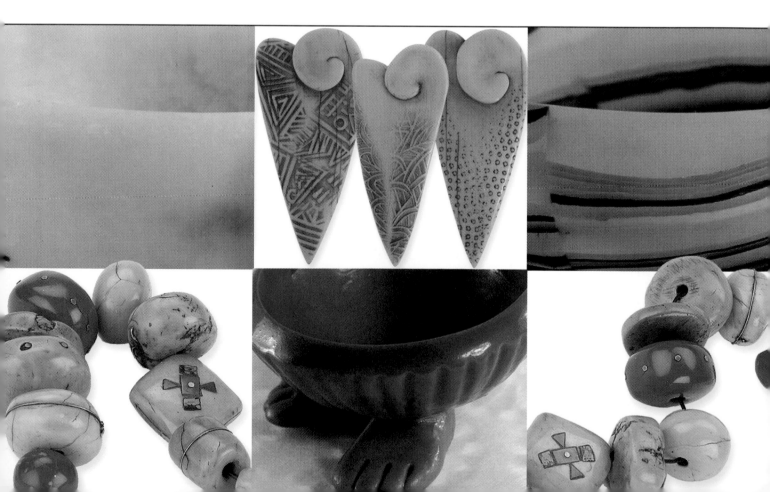

chapter 5

# introductory projects

# imitating
# turquoise

Turquoise has been treasured for centuries. Conjuring up the vitality of clear sky and clean water, cultures throughout the world love turquoise for its unique color and associations. Imagine the thrill of digging through dirt and rock and finding a stone as blue as the sky!

Turquoise has a large component of copper, and its distinctive blue-green color arises from the same mineral reactions that cause the blue-green patina on copper roofs. Turquoise usually has some degree of matrix—darker lines or areas of material around the turquoise itself. This can vary from occasional, delicate lines to large areas of brownish-black or rubbly grey.

To re-create turquoise in polymer clay, first consider it as coming in three styles: no matrix, fine lines of matrix, and large areas of matrix. These three styles require different techniques. In this book you will learn how to duplicate an irregular, nuggetlike turquoise with fine lines of matrix.

Turquoise has a wider range of color than the bright sky blue often seen. Its color can range through most blues and blue-greens, dark teals, and brownish greens. There's even a chartreuse turquoise. There is very little color variation within an individual piece of turquoise. All nuggets are the same color and any different colors arise from staining on the surface of the stone in areas that absorb oils or minerals unevenly.

Turquoise is an opaque, fairly soft stone, which easily absorbs the oils from human hands. Older cherished beads, especially from the Himalayas, are known for their rich patina, an effect you can achieve by staining your beads with acrylic paint, then buffing them.

Turquoise re-creations are dependant on generating small polymer clay nuggets, then consolidating them to mimic the bumpy surface of the original. This is accomplished by chopping turquoise mix in a food processor. Chapter 4 addresses how to control the size and shape of the chopped bits, which determine the look of the final re-creation.

Surface characteristics—the tactile and visual texture—of turquoise pieces are dependant on the degree of matrix and whatever shaping of the stone you wish to imply. American turquoise has often been rounded to a gentle cabachon, whereas Asian turquoise is likely to be the organic shape of the original stone. The matrix is revealed when the stone has been carved and shaped and its interior structure becomes visible.

Applying a patina will bring out whatever matrix you created, and polishing will bring up the color. Let's begin!

The restorative colors of turquoise conjure up the magical beauty of sky and water.

## new techniques

making polymer nuggets

painting and dusting for organic effect

sanding, painting, and buffing

simple necklace stringing and working with findings

# turquoise beads

## instructions

*1* Condition the light turquoise and white clays together thoroughly into a solid pale turquoise color.

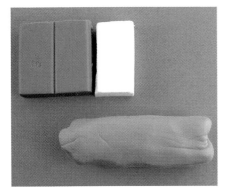

*2* Chop this turquoise color into little nuggets in the food processor. For small, angular nuggets of polymer clay, use stiff clay, or chill the clay and blade in the freezer before chopping. For larger, rounded nuggets, use warmer, softer clay.

*3* Gently shape clumps of these nuggets into beads. Classic turquoise beads are often irregularly shaped, showing off their natural state. Create an assemblage of shapes that you will enjoy when strung together. Chop and reshape any shapes you don't like.

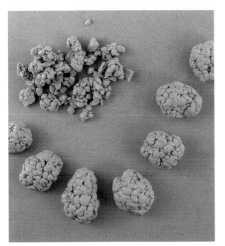

If the polymer clay is very soft, wear latex gloves to avoid embossing fingerprints into the polymer. After baking, any fingerprints will have to be sanded away.

*4* If the polymer clay body is quite soft, you may lose definition between the nuggets as you shape the beads. If this happens, put 1/2 cup cornstarch in a small plastic bag. Place one of the beads in the bag and gently shake it. The cornstarch will lightly fill in the crevices between the nuggets. Cornstarch prevents polymer clay from sticking to itself. Even if you press the polymer clay beads together, the cornstarch will now prevent the clay from reconsolidating along those lines between the nuggets. Those crevices will then trap the paint applied later. **Note:** *If the clay body is stiff, this step isn't necessary.*

*5* When the beads are the shape you want, gently pierce a hole in each one. Pierce the hole from both ends so there is a rounded contour to each opening.

*6* Set the beads on a nest of polyfill if available, and bake in a preheated oven for 30 minutes. The polyfill supports the polymer clay while the unbaked

## for this introductory project, you will need:

Fimo Classic
   2 ounces light turquoise (#32)
   1 ounce white (#0)
acrylic paint: burnt umber
fine dirt or dust
jewelry cord
silver beads or substitute
necklace clasp
crimp beads
polyfill
old toothbrush

The materials you'll need to make a necklace of turquoise beads: polymer clays, paint, a bit of fine dust or dirt, optional silver beads, jewelry cord, and necklace findings.

**Note:** *Detailed information on basic polymer clay techniques can be found in Chapter 4, Foundation Processes.*

clay gets soft and slumps slightly in the heat. Remove and let cool.

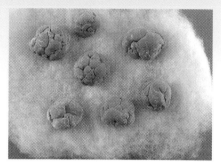

**7** Sand the beads with 400-grit wet-or-dry sandpaper, then repeat with 600-grit. Be sure to do the sanding under water.

**8** Rub burnt umber acrylic paint on each bead. Use an old toothbrush to poke the paint into deep areas. Bright blue crevices look very artificial on an antique turquoise bead. **Note:** *Acrylic paint will stain your clothes if not immediately washed out, so wear an old shirt when doing techniques with toothbrushes and paint.*

**9** Rub a bit of fine dust or dirt over the wet paint with your fingertips and brush off the excess. The dirt will be held permanently when cured on the paint's surface. A fine coating of dust mattes the paint, adding a hint of age to the beads, making them look old and well-handled.

**10** Wipe excess surface paint gently away with a very slightly damp paper towel until the beads look good to you. Too much water on the paper towel will rinse all the paint off the bead. Put the beads back in the oven for 10 minutes to set the paint. Remove and let cool.

**11** For delicate adjustments to the paint after setting it, lightly sand with a very fine (at least 1200- or 1500-grit) wet-or-dry sandpaper. Areas sanded with such fine grit sandpaper will polish up quickly to a high gloss. Use this for areas that would be polished by handling if this were a true turquoise bead.

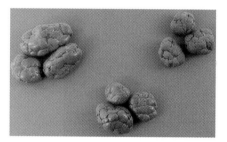

The beads in the upper right have been painted and dusted; polished versions are shown below in the center. More paint was removed from the surface of the beads in the upper left.

**12** Lay the beads out, designing a 28" necklace. Using a cord that will not abrade or stretch, alternate turquoise beads with very simple silver spherical beads, then add four extra silver beads on either side after the turquoise. Finish the necklace to 28", filling in with small silver-colored beads. Select the clasp you wish to use.

**13** After stringing the full set of beads you have chosen, slide a crimp bead on the cord. Slip the cord through one loop of the clasp and run the cord back through the crimp bead and back through at least 1" of the final beads.

**14** Squeeze the crimp bead shut with needle-nose pliers. This collapses the bead sharply down onto the cord, pinning the cord in place. Repeat on the other side of the necklace.

**15** Clip off the extra length of cord. That's it!

### note

*The details of assembling components, choosing cord and findings, and connecting cord and findings are outside the scope of this book. However, many excellent books on bead stringing are available and most bead stores happily give information on making necklaces. Take advantage of these sources to give yourself a solid knowledge from which you can develop your own unique approaches to necklace design.*

A necklace using beads begun with the same formula as our project beads, but with more paint left on the surface before setting, light sanding, and polishing.

# imitating lapis

Ah, the rich deep blue of lapis lazuli! Lapis conjures up ancient Egypt, precious ultramarine stones inlaid on golden sarcophagi, exotic luxuries from time out of mind. Always prized for its stunning color, true lapis, like the other stones imitated here, has an aristocratic heritage. Originally from Afghanistan and traded throughout the ancient world, it is still mined, cut, and traded today. The gold or silver glimmers are iron pyrites in the rock.

Imitating lapis is a good introductory exercise. Analyze its color. How do the color variations appear? Lapis is similar to turquoise, another stone with a visible crystal structure that must be reproduced to accurately mimic the material. Lapis' crystals are small and angular, unlike the rounded turquoise nuggets. You will develop the fine lapis mix by chopping by hand.

Most lapis is actually several very closely related dark blues together. Only the rarest lapis is a single pure color, with no variation or metallic flecking. If you like, after observing high-quality lapis, try mixing this pure blue on your own, then follow the rest of the steps on pages 79-80, judging for yourself which lapis you like best. An odd fact about the imitative techniques is that if you mimic a flawless specimen of a material, it tends to look artificial. True high-quality stones, free of all imperfections, are rarely seen. However, imitators of these materials make ersatz replicas of those flawless high-quality stones rather than of the idiosyncratic, slightly imperfect versions. There are many more flawless fakes than flawless originals, and so we associate flawlessness with artificiality.

After looking at original pieces of a material, you'll have a feel for the personality of the material. Re-create based on the personality, not on one specific piece. In lapis, the fine angularity of the grains, the occasional metallic shiver, the deep opaque blue tones– these are its personality. Use those as the basis for the re-creation.

The projects are made with lapis with some matrix and some metallic flecking to teach you all the variations at once. The blues of the clay bodies should be very close in color. Lapis itself is opaque, but its matrix, when present, is normally a semitranslucent grey-white. Color and opacity are simple to create in this imitative. In true lapis, the metallic flecking is an associated mineral called pyrite, sometimes called fools' gold. It can appear silver or gold. Metallic leaf will mimic this effect. Lapis is a harder stone, and usually left smooth, so it will be easy to mimic these surface characteristics in a polymer version. Let's give it a try!

Lapis lazuli, with its occasional glints of gold or silver, invites us into its depth and strength of color.

## new techniques

chopping and mixing by hand

adding metallic foils into the clay

carving and backfilling with unbaked clay

working with decorative wire

folding paper to make an accordion book (page 112)

# lapis lazuli
## bird earrings

## instructions

*1* Mix together 1/2 ounce each of blue and ultramarine. When finished, you will have one ounce of a blue between blue and ultramarine. You'll still have a remaining ounce each of unconditioned blue and unconditioned ultramarine.

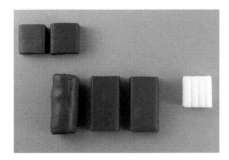

*2* Use a tissue blade to chop up the three blue clay bodies together into roughly 1/8" grains. Mix them thoroughly together as you chop, creating a finely chopped tricolor blue mix. If the mixed blue clay is much softer than the two packaged blues, let it stiffen before you chop the clays together so the grains all look similar.

*3* Chop the translucent clay into this blue mixture, mixing the clays together as you dice. The translucent should be small, but varying in size rather than all about the same size. Lapis can also be made without the translucent clay.

*4* Add the gold leaf. Lay the sheet on top of the chopped clay, fold some of the polymer mixture onto the leaf to hold it down, and begin chopping. Keep folding and chopping the gold leaf into the blue mixture until the leaf fragments are about 3/16" to 1/8" in size. The finer you chop the leaf, the more subtle the areas of gold will be in your final object.

There is a reason for chopping in sequence, rather than just chopping everything together at one time. As you chop, the grains you create get smaller and smaller. The blue grains in the lapis should be quite small and thoroughly mixed. Chopping them up three times does this without great effort.

The milky translucent areas should be small, random, and spread out. In true lapis these are random imperfections. If the

## for this introductory project, you will need:

Fimo Classic
   1-1/2 ounces ultramarine (#33)
   1-1/2 ounces blue (#37)
   1/2 ounce Art Translucent (#00)
   pinch of yellow
gold composite metallic leaf
2" length of 20-gauge silver wire
pair sterling ear wires

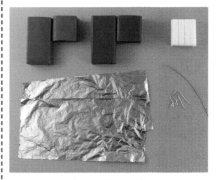

The materials used in making earrings of imitative lapis: polymer clays in two closely related colors of blue, translucent polymer, and a sheet of composite gold leaf make the lapis itself. Yellow polymer defines the eyes of the birds. The 20-gauge wire, earring findings, and glue transform the lapis pieces into earrings.

**Note:** *Detailed information on basic polymer clay techniques can be found in Chapter 4, Foundation Processes.*

translucent clay is mixed consistently throughout the blue clay body, you will have just created a dark blue translucent clay. Lapis is not a translucent stone. Some true lapis is flawless–a solid blue color–but there isn't much flawless lapis lazuli, so an imitation of flawless lapis tends to look unreal. Ironically, slight irregularities make for easier recognition.

The composite gold leaf fragments need to be large enough to be visible in the finished piece. Chopping the leaf up from the beginning would make it so fine that it would be almost invisible.

5 Form a pancake of lapis grains with your fingers, then roll over to flatten it with a glass. The edges of the pancake must be as tightly packed as the central area, so keep pushing in from the sides as you flatten.

In this step you are making enough raw flat lapis stock to use for other projects. The pancake should be about 3/16" thick and cohesive enough for you to lift up from the work surface, turn over, check the other side, and lay back down.

6 Cut out a paper pattern as a template for the birds. Use the one on page 141 or create your own design.

7 Using a sharp X-acto blade, cut out two birds. Gently smooth the edges a little, pushing back any stray lapis grains that crumble off.

8 Press small holes in either side of the birds' heads, where you'd like the eyes to go. (I used a ballpoint pen tip for these round holes.) Make sure the holes match from side to side of the bird, and from bird to bird. The contour and size of the holes will determine how the finished eyes look. Set tiny balls of opaque golden yellow clay in the holes. Later, you'll sand the yellow clay flush with the surface.

9 Make two 1/4" long eye pins from 20-gauge silver wire. Set one into the top margin of each bird. If putting the eye pins in distorts the shape of the birds, press the clay back into place.

10 Bake in a preheated oven for 20 minutes. Remove and let cool.

11 Pull the eye pins out of the baked birds.

12 Sand the birds under water with 400-grit, then 600-grit wet-or-dry sandpaper.

13 To easily buff the birds to the traditional high shine of lapis, sand the birds again with 1000- or 1200-grit wet-or-dry sandpaper. The finer the final grit sandpaper you use, the higher shine you will get after polishing.

14 Using Zap-a-Gap, glue the eye pins back into the birds. Make sure the glue is dry before you handle the birds for the next step.

15 Polish the birds. With such small objects, pay special attention to keeping your fingers away from where you just polished. Hold one bird securely in one place, buff everywhere you can without moving your fingers, then put that bird down to cool and buff the other. Repeat this until both are buffed everywhere.

Polishing the polymer clay temporarily heats the surface and warm polymer is sensitive to texture. Your tightly gripped fingertips will emboss the surface of the birds. Let the piece cool for just a minute to avoid this.

16 The last step. Add sterling ear wires to turn these beautiful birds into a pair of dangling lapis lazuli earrings. Charming!

# imitating
# jade

Slightly translucent, jade can be any color from cool milky white through endless nuances of green, blue, lavender, yellow, and even brown and black. Colors that vary within the same piece have always attracted collectors.

In some jade, the crystalline structure of the stone is visible and in others, there is no visual texture. Jade is one of the hardest stones to work, and usually takes the form of smooth pieces with shallow incising or carving, rather than any elaborate relief. What is referred to as jade can be either of two stones–jadeite or nephrite. Darker green colors result from iron in the stone, and there are various surface colorations like white chalky patches or reddish staining. Jade is treasured worldwide even now; glossy bracelets with different shadowing colors encircle many a wrist.

Often, imitations of flawless material specimens look artificial, and this is particularly true of jade. Ersatz jade imitations in pure bright green (mimicking the apple-green jade prized by Chinese emperors) are common plastic gewgaws.

For more natural realism, you will create a mottled, uneven array of colors on the piece. Laying colors together in a random array is good practice for letting go of your brain's desire for patterning, of a pre-determined idea of how things should look. The more random the markings, the more realistic your imitative jade will look.

To imitate jade, you will develop a translucent-based clay body. Translucent polymer clays are similar to jade's degree of translucency,

so by mixing a green clay and using it to tint the translucent polymer, you create a clay body that will look much like the jade once baked. To encourage you to experiment with different brands of translucent clays, you will use both the Fimo and Prēmo translucents in one project. The difference will show up after baking, once the clays have polymerized and the internal pebbling of the Fimo contrasts to the lack thereof in the Prēmo.

The projects in this book include a common range of colors. Colors in jade blend together, rather than appearing as sharply defined veining or areas. You will mix and use at least three different translucent-based colors in the jade projects and you will learn a technique to feather the colors into each other for a realistic soft blending of color.

The surface of jade pieces tends to be simple and highly polished. Most imitative jade is not painted. However, the pale, dusty patina on some jade can be mimicked by judicious painting. Also, incised central and south American jades often have red oxide rubbed into the markings, and you can do likewise. Sanding and polishing will dramatically alter your jade's appearance, so remember not to judge your piece until after you've done the final steps!

Jade's silky translucency and coolness has always been coveted. Polymer clay's qualities truly let you re-create the beauties of this precious, timeless material.

## new techniques

translucent clay body mixing

feathering

baking on forms

decorative line carving and painting (page 121)

# three-color jade bowl

# instructions

*1* Divide the green clay into three equal sections. Each third will be the base of a variation of green. Mix the first third with 1/32 ounce each (almost a sliver) of ultramarine and purple. Mix the next third with 1/4 ounce golden yellow, creating a warmer, brighter green. Leave the last section in its original leaf green state. Condition and mix all three clay bodies completely.

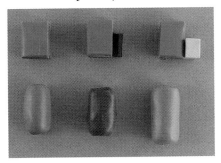

These three green clay bodies are like dye pots from which you will take tiny pinches of color to add to the translucent clay. Since there is no pigment at all in translucent clay, even a small amount of colored clay will tint it.

*2* Take a ball the size of a small green pea (a petit pois) from the original leaf green. Mix it completely into one ounce of Art Translucent. This will give you a very pale green clay body. Set it aside.

Take a slightly larger ball (classic garden pea size) from the gold-green clay. Mix this thoroughly into 1/2 ounce Art Translucent. Set it aside.

Take a ball the same garden pea size of the blue and purple-green clay and mix it thoroughly into 1/2 ounce of Prēmo translucent with bleach. Set it aside.

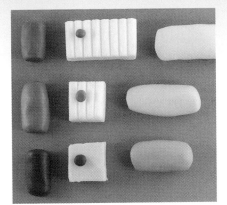

Fimo Art Translucent has a beautiful, pebbly appearance after baking. Prēmo translucent with bleach has a very homogenous appearance after baking. When used together on the same piece, the contrast of the noncrystalline and the pebbly appearance mimics the natural variation in true stone.

*3* From each of these three translucent-based clay bodies, make a dime-size piece. Bake all three samples in a preheated oven for 10 minutes. Remove and let cool.

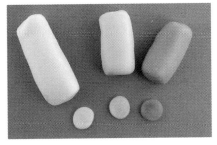

Translucent clay has no pigment or opacifier in it (it looks white wax in the package). Before baking, a tinted translucent clay body looks like the pastel version of whatever color was mixed in because of the apparent whiteness of the clay. After baking, that whiteness shifts (polymerizes) so the base clay body is now translucent. The added color shows up more and the baked clay is darker and more vivid. All translucent-based colors exhibit some color shift after baking.

## for this introductory project, you will need:

Fimo
  1 ounce green (#5)
  1/4 ounce golden yellow (#16)
  1/32 ounce ultramarine #(33)
  1/32 ounce purple (#6)
  1-1/2 ounces Art Translucent (#00)
  1/2 ounce black (#9)
Prēmo
  1/2 ounce translucent with bleach (#5310)
light bulb

The materials needed for the three-color jade bowl: nothing other than polymer clay and a light bulb as a form is required to produce this little bowl.

**Note:** *Detailed information on basic polymer clay techniques can be found in Chapter 4, Foundation Processes.*

Always bake a sample of a translucent-based color before using it in a project. After seeing the effect of this color shift design, adjust the mix and bake another sample. After decades of working in polymer clay, I still bake test pieces of all my translucent-based colors.

Check the baked samples. They're all going to make up the same bowl—do you like their interaction? If you want to change the color of any of these clay bodies, this is the time. Remember to bake a test sample of any changes you make.

4 Roll the lightest green clay into a ball. Using your fingers, gently flatten the ball into a circle of clay about earlobe thickness. Roll gently over the circle with a glass to smooth it (make the clay smoother, not thinner).

Shape the darker green clay into a rough half circle, also earlobe thickness. Smooth this with a glass as well.

Trim the dark half circle to about a third circle. Trim the pale full circle to the complementary section—about two-thirds circle—so the two pieces together would make a complete circle.

5 Pinch the straight edge of each of the sections into a fine, thin wedge, preparatory to feathering them together. This tapered wedge should be about 1/4" to 1/2" wide. If you have not feathered polymer clays together before, refer to page 54 for instructions. Pull the tip of the taper with your fingertips until it stretches and tears apart, creating a very thin clay at the edge.

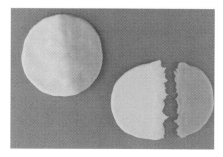

6 Lay the tapered edge of the darker green section over the corresponding edge of the pale green section. Overlap the clays completely, making a thicker seam along the joint. Pinch from both the obverse and reverse sides of the disc, fusing the sections together securely along this seam. Maintain an even overall thickness of clay. Both the obverse and reverse of this disc will show in the final project (as the inside and outside of the bowl) so treat both sides equally throughout this process.

7 For this next step, the polymer clay must be sticking to an immobile surface. If you are working on a surface that shifts under you, stick it down now. Position the polymer circle about a foot in from the edge of the table on your work surface. Press the circle down so it sticks to the surface. The distance gives you room to move your arm comfortably while stroking across the polymer circle.

8 Use the broad side of your thumb (not the tip of your finger, which would dent the clay) to brush across the blend on the surface of the circle. This will pull the top color out even thinner across the underlying color. Create a soft fade from one color to the other (refer to page 54). Your goal is to develop a smooth transition from one color to another, with no line separating the two colors of green. Repeat on the reverse side. The proportion of dark to pale color will be different on this side. Not to worry, it's supposed to look this way.

9 Pinch off a small shape from the gold-green translucent mix. Make a pod shape. Taper its edges out by pinching and pulling until the shape is about 1/8" thick in the center and very fine along its edges. Press this shape onto the circle. Position it so that when you feather it you brush in the same direction as you feathered the pale green. Otherwise, you'll be feathering against the joint you already established and will rough up the previous fade of colors. Press the gold-green shape down in the center first, then roll your finger over it from the center all the way out to the edges to firmly fuse the clays together.

Finish the feathering process by brushing out the edges of the streak, softening the transition between the colors. Repeat with another small piece of gold-green translucent clay. Be careful to maintain an even thickness in the original circle of clay. There is a tendency for the underlying polymer clay to thin out as you feather over the surface.

10 Optional: This optional step will create the appearance of imperfections such as the random minerals that might have been present in the crystalline soup of jade, but are not themselves jade.

Break apart a block of stiff black polymer clay. Rub the broken edges of the clay pieces together over a clear spot on your work surface to get crumbles or flecks of black clay. If the black clay is too soft to crumble, find a different clay.

Being very random in your approach, press an area of the polymer circle onto some of the black flecks, then turn the circle over and repeat. Be very sparing with this technique. Impurities in true jade are very random; there may be only one or two imperfections in a piece.

Roll gently over the surface to press the flecks into the polymer and smooth out your fingerprints. Avoid thinning the polymer circle itself. Later you will have to sand away any fingerprints that remain.

**11** Use a circle cutter to cut a 3-1/2" circle from the blended polymer clay circle. Leave the circle on your work surface while you remove the excess clay from around the cutter. Avoid picking up and distorting the circle.

**12** Sand or scrub the numbers from the top of a standard light bulb. If you don't remove them, faint backward lettering will appear on the inside of the bowl. Center the glass end of the light bulb in the middle of the clay circle. Press down lightly, adhering the bulb to the clay and embossing a flat spot on the underside of the clay that will be the base of the bowl.

**13** Gently ease the clay up onto the sides of the bulb. To simplify this, select any section of clay that does not touch the bulb and press halfway across this section against the bulb, then press the halfway point of each of those two sections against the bulb. Repeat this until the clay evenly contacts the bulb. Maintain an even thickness of clay against the bulb but don't worry about the irregular upper margins of the clay. Press the clay securely against the bulb, working out any air bubbles so the inside evenly adapts that shiny glass texture during baking.

**14** You will be baking the polymer clay on the light bulb. To successfully remove the baked polymer bowl from the light bulb, the bowl's upper edge must be at the widest dimension of the bulb. Once the bowl starts to taper in on the bulb, you won't be able to get the bulb out without breaking the glass. Stand the bulb up on that flat spot you created. Rotate the bulb on its base and mark the widest point of the bowl by scribing or making light cuts.

**15** Trim all the way around the bulb, checking to make sure you are still cutting at that widest spot, and not going up or down. Take your time: you can always take more off but it's hard to put clay back on. Remove excess clay above the widest point of the bulb.

**16** Set the flat base of the bowl on a small piece of paper and bake the light bulb and polymer clay bowl together for 20 minutes in a preheated oven. Remove and let cool.

**17** When the polymer has completely cooled, pull the baked bowl off the bulb. Baked polymer will not fuse to glass so if the bowl feels stuck, it's just a bit of suction. Don't worry, just keep working on it. If necessary, insert the tip of a knitting needle between the baked polymer and the glass, being careful not to scratch the polymer. I usually keep going around and around the bulb, gently pulling the clay down bit by bit until it slips off the bulb. (The shiny interior of the bowl is the impression of the glossy smoothness of the glass light bulb. How convenient!)

**18** Under water, sand the outside of the bowl, using 400-, 600-, then 1000- and 1500-grit wet-or-dry sandpaper. Before doing any wet-or-dry sanding, if you have a belt sander, bevel the outer edge of the bowl by rotating the upper edge against the sander, as I did. This adds a subtle, refined feel to the bowl.

**19** Buff the outside of the bowl. Beautiful. Stand it up and let the light shine through. That's it!

# imitating coral

Coral's rich orange-red tones have been used for desirable beads for centuries. Slight color variations from bead to bead exhibit authenticity in a strand of these luscious marine gems.

Coral is actually the structures built by marine organisms, their architecture. True coral occurs in a range of beautiful reds, pinks, oranges, and even black. Horn corals, related creatures, also grow in blues, greens, and metallic golds.

Coral glows because of that slight luminosity or depth of color inherent in almost all organic materials. When you duplicate these materials, it's important to add translucency into the clay body to develop that luminosity, or the coral will look flat and lifeless. Another aspect of coral common to other natural materials is its range of closely related colors, bead to bead, rather than one consistent color for all beads. We are so immersed in the millions of colors that wash across our visual field constantly that we tend to tune out all that variation –until we see something that is one solid color and realize how artificial it looks. Nothing in nature is a solid flat color. For the coral bead project, you will make three close coral-red colors and add a small amount of translucent.

The external surface on coral depends on its production. Much coral is left with some of the natural textures from growth processes showing. Some beads are completely shaped and smooth. You will mimic the effect of organic processes on smooth root coral beads by embossing textures to simulate both the coral's structure and random pitting that occurs on coral.

The patina on coral is designed to bring up that rich color and luminosity, and all corals are polished to some degree. You'll do that, and then string your beads in a simple, effective necklace.

## new techniques

creating a range of related colors

striating the clay with translucent

texturing with fine gravel

# *coral bead necklace*

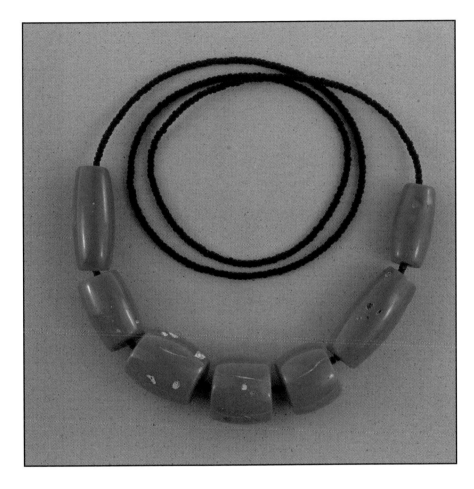

## for this introductory project, you will need:

polymer clay
    1/4 ounce white (#0)
    1/4 ounce Indian red (#24)
    1/2 ounce golden yellow (#16)
    1 ounce Art Translucent (#00)
acrylic paint
    white or off-white
    burnt umber
pale ash if available
small black seed beads
Beadalon, Softflex or similar
    stringing cord
crimp bead

The materials necessary to make a coral bead necklace: polymer clays, white or off-white and burnt umber acrylic paint, small black beads, and bead-stringing material like Beadalon. You will make a long necklace.

***Note:*** *Detailed information on basic polymer clay techniques can be found in Chapter 4, Foundation Processes.*

## instructions

*1* Mix a coral-red clay body using one ounce Indian red, one ounce golden yellow, and 1/2 ounce of white. Set this aside. Condition the translucent clay and set that aside also.

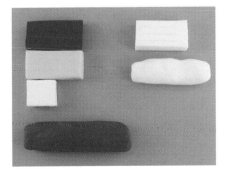

**2** Divide the coral mix into three sections. You will vary it by adding small amounts of different colors to each section, creating three slightly different tints of coral-red polymer clay. Colors in coral vary, like all organic materials. A coral necklace will look more realistic if the beads are slightly different tints.

**3** To one section of the coral-red clay, thoroughly mix in the remaining 1/2 ounce of yellow. To another section, thoroughly mix in the remaining 1/4 ounce of golden yellow. To the last section, thoroughly mix in 1/4 ounce of true red. Set these three mixes aside. These coral-red variations are the base colors of your beads.

**4** Make a snake of the coral red about as thick as your thumb. Make several very thin strings of the translucent, about the thinness of spaghetti. These strands can be uneven but must be thin. Pull the clay out to make these: as it stretches it gets thinner.

**5** Lay the thin translucent strands along the length of the red snake, around the clay, as shown. Press the translucent strands onto the red clay, so they are affixed in place.

**6** Pull out this striped snake, cut it in half, and consolidate the halves into a snake with finer translucent stripes along its sides.

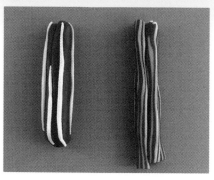

**7** Repeat once or twice more. In the final stage, the translucent stripes should still be visible, about the scale of 18-gauge wire or a thick buttonhole twist, whichever simile you prefer. Stop when the stripes are still visible but fairly fine. Repeat this translucent veining on the other two colors of coral you mixed, so that you have three slightly different colors, each with veining.

**8** Decide what size beads you want on your necklace. A range of sizes usually looks more authentic, since coral is precious. Only for more expensive sets of beads would overly large beads be shaved down to match smaller ones. Divide the striped coral-red snakes into segments of the size beads you want. These are your proto-beads. Do not smooth the seams that resulted from the pulling and reconsolidating (these grooves will smooth somewhat in the next steps, and will look natural in the final beads).

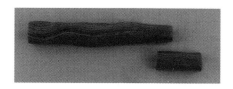

**9** You may leave your coral as it is now or add one or both

of the following two surface variations to some of the beads. For the ones you're leaving as is, skip to step 12.

**10** The first variation creates the occasional milky freckle or blotch you see on coral. Break apart an unconditioned block of Art Translucent. Rub the two rough ends together over your work surface to generate flecks of translucent clay. This technique mimics natural eccentricities in the way the coral grows. Roll the proto-bead over a few of the flecks. Be sparing and random in their placement on the bead. Sometimes even one is good enough. Roll the bead back and forth on a clean surface to fuse the flecks into the coral clay. If the polymer thins out or distorts as you are rolling, just squeeze it back to the correct shape once the flecks look as if they are part of the coral clay.

**11** The second variation mimics the pitting that sometimes appears on coral from worm damage. To add this texture to your beads, get a small dish of fine gravel or sandy dirt (rounded grains are best). Sprinkle a tiny amount of this on your work surface. Insert a needle tool or knitting needle into one of the beads and lightly roll over the fine gravel. You are embossing, not

embedding. Do not push too hard. As with the translucent flecks, be sparing and random with this.

**12** Pierce holes in the beads with a needle tool. Remember to go in from each end, so that the edge of the hole is smooth.

**13** You may choose to put flecks alone on some beads, flecks and a texture on some, texture alone on others, and leave some plain. When finished, you should have an assortment of beads ready to be baked.

**14** Bake the coral beads in a preheated oven for 20 to 30 minutes. Because of the pure Art Translucent areas in coral, baking longer is not recommended. The translucent may yellow a bit and become less realistic in appearance. Remove and let cool.

**15** Under water, sand the coral with 400- and 600-grit wet-or-dry sandpaper. Sand the ends down to flatten any puffy, rounded contour at the ends of the beads. Coral itself is a hard material, which is cut into sections and polished. Mimic that effect with your sanding.

**16** Mix the burnt umber and off-white acrylic paints to a light brown and rub paint into all the textures on the beads. The fine grooves that remain from the folds and seams will hold a little paint, and the pits will

take more. Then rub some of the fine ash or pale dirt across the textured areas, dulling the paint as it dries and adding a little more aged feeling to the beads.

**17** When the paint is dry, polish the beads.

**18** Arrange the beads in a pleasing manner and string them on the cord. Add two small black beads between each coral bead. Start stringing from the central coral bead (or whichever coral bead has a large hole). Go up one side, add on all the small black beads, and go back down the other side, so the cord ends between the central beads.

**19** Wherever a coral bead's hole is much bigger than the small black beads, and the coral bead slides over the black beads easily, string enough black beads onto the cord so that they run all along inside the coral bead. When the coral bead shifts, there will always be black beads beneath, and the necklace will hang better as well.

**20** To finish this longer necklace, use a crimp bead to join the ends of the cord and hide the joint inside the central coral bead. To do this, first make sure the necklace is the length you want, fitting easily over your head. Allow a couple extra inches of cord on either end. Read the rest of these direc-

tions first, to familiarize yourself with this neat trick.

**21** Add a crimp bead at the end of the string. Slide the other end of the cord through it as well. This should occur right next to that large, central bead with the big hole.

**22** Pull the cord taut and squash the crimp bead. If you do this right, the gap should be as wide as the pliers that closed the crimp bead. Now wiggle the large coral bead over the crimp bead and play with the necklace until it is all hanging fluidly. Voila.

# imitating amber

Rich and exotic, the allure of amber began with the Egyptians and continues today.

Did you know that amber has been gathered from the beaches of the Baltic Sea for at least 10,000 years? Ancient Egyptians, Greeks, Romans, Hebrews, Mayans—every culture—valued amber, a type of fossilized resin that includes myrrh and frankincense, as well as copal and the amber we usually imagine. True amber is resin that seeped out of a pine tree millions of years ago, folding and twisting and dripping over itself and eventually falling to the ground, polymerizing and fossilizing. What a rich heritage you are sharing as you use one polymer to mimic another!

Natural amber ranges in color from a frothy pale blueish-white, through beautiful warm yellows, saffrons, browns, and reds. Amber can also range in translucency, from truly transparent to opaque. Because of the dripping, swirling viscosity of the resin as it seeps out of the tree, swirls of very closely related colors and translucencies are visible in most amber. Almost all natural materials are more complex and varied than you could reasonably reproduce, and the eccentricities in amber give that sense of rich natural beauty that a homogenous material cannot.

An amber necklace will be more visually interesting, as well as more realistic, if the colors of the beads vary. Variation is a hallmark of nature, and the natural formation of amber—sap oozing out of a tree, dripping down the side of the bark, mixing with various materials, lying on the forest floor for decades—pushes variation to the edge. So vary the way you make your amber beads. Even more than the other imitative techniques, there is no wrong way to make amber.

Polymer clay is not yet available in a truly transparent version, but you can come close to mimicking a translucent appearance. You will re-create the type of amber often seen as large beads in African or Himalayan adornments, usually from those Baltic amber deposits. This amber is a variegated rich yellow: if you look at it closely, you'll see those swirls of different colors mentioned above.

This effect is straightforward to re-create in polymer. By mixing similar colors of yellow, then mixing those partially with plain translucent clay, a baked bead will have the same organic feel as the original. A reminder: remember to consciously look closely at anything you want to re-create. Subtle visual signals about a material are being picked up by your brain even if you haven't noticed them. To imitate something well, those subtle clues must be added.

Amber can easily be worked; it's a soft material that does not hold delicate detail particularly well. So the shapes of amber beads and objects tend to be softened themselves, and surface details are usually shallow if present. Since amber has always been regarded as valuable, the shapes of these objects often followed the contours of the original piece, so that all of the material could be used. An organic, hand-shaped feel to amber beads and objects was the result.

Amber has roughly the same weight as polymer clay, since it is a polymerized resin itself. Because of that, this re-creation is more like its original than any of the other imitative techniques.

# amber beads

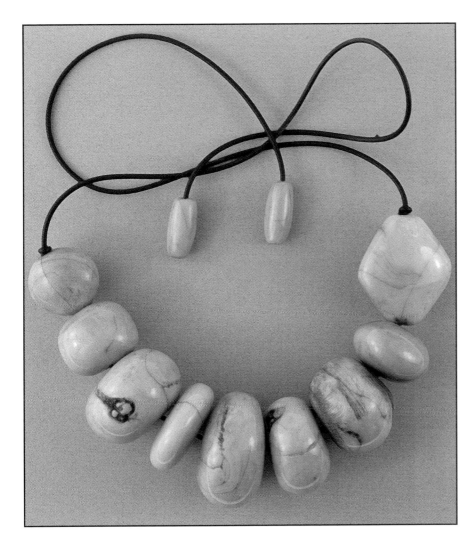

for this introductory
project, you will need:

Fimo
  1 ounce classic golden yellow
  (#16)
  1/2 ounce light turquoise (#32)
  1/2 ounce classic Art
  Translucent (#00)
  1/8 ounce classic bordeaux
  (#23)
Cernit
  1 ounce yellow (#021)
Prēmo
  1/2 ounce translucent with
  bleach (#5310)
acrylic paint: burnt umber

The materials you'll need to make a
necklace of amber beads: polymer
clay in yellows, translucents, and
bordeaux, acrylic paint, turquoise
clay to make a few small nuggets,
and black rubber cord to string the
beads.

**Note:** *Detailed information on
basic polymer clay techniques can
be found in Chapter 4, Foundation
Processes.*

## instructions

*1* True amber swirls together a range of golden yellows. To achieve this, you will create similarly colored clay bodies. Cut the yellow Fimo, Cernit, and translucent Prēmo into 1/2 ounce segments. Make two identical collections, each containing 1/2 ounce Fimo yellow, 1/2 ounce Cernit

yellow, and 1/2 ounce Prēmo translucent. Keep the Fimo Art Translucent aside. Do not condition or mix it in yet.

*2* Add a rice-size grain of bordeaux to one collection of yellow and translucent clays. Mix these clays into a light saffron yellow color. Add a small pea-size grain of bordeaux to the other collection of clays and mix it into a medium saffron yellow color. (Fimo bordeaux is a very strong color, extremely saturated with pigment. Even tiny bits will richly tint clay bodies. Be very sparing with it until you're used to its strength.)

**3** Roll each yellow clay body into a snake. Condition the Art Translucent and roll it into a snake as well.

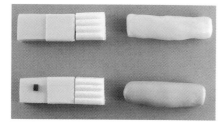

**4** Cut the three snakes in half and bundle the six snake sections together, alternating the colors as you lay them together. As you squeeze them, pull and stretch them out until the new bundle is a variegated snake about the length of the original snake.

**5** Cut this new snake in half. Bundle and stretch it out again, as in the last step. You may twist the amber snake once: amber's streaks of color turn and fall back on themselves and random swirls in moderation add realism. This technique is similar to the one for creating ivory, but not as painstaking.

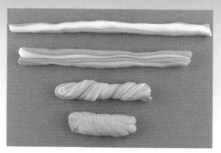

**6** You may stop now or cut the bundle again and recombine it. Maintain some visible streaking. This stage is finished when the lines are fine but visible, with some swirling. Don't inadvertently mix the clay into a solid color. Amber varies tremendously from piece to piece, so it's wise to look at the real thing and decide how you want yours to appear.

**7** Stretch the amber stock out and pull off 10 segments between the size of a walnut and a big hazelnut. Set aside the smallest segment.

**8** Segment by segment, gently roll out the clay, then twist and fold it back on itself to create a thick, knotted ball of amber. Be loose. Continue until you've made nine knotted balls.

**9** Return to the smallest segment and cut it in half. Fold and twist each half into a small bead.

**10** Wear latex gloves for the next few steps to prevent fingerprints. Gently round each knotted ball into a smooth shape. Allow the folds and seams of the knots to remain (these will trap paint later, adding realism). The bead shapes can be organic and irregular such as spheres, lentils, pillows. I made one fat diamond-shaped bead by flattening a sphere gently into a thick square shape, then refining that into a diamond. Also smooth the two little beads.

**11** Use a knitting needle to pierce large holes in each bead. Pierce from both the top and bottom to round the edges of the hole. If possible, do not pierce the two tubular beads all the way through as these will later be glued on the ends of the cord.

**12** Now it's time to add surface variation. Before beginning, read steps 13 through 16 and decide how much you want to do. Surface textures show up much more after baking, when paint has been applied to the bead. Go easy on texturing until you have finished a bead completely–including polishing–and until you understand how the markings translate to a finished piece. Leave at least one bead untouched as a comparison.

**13** Use the rough edge of a piece of bark to texture the unbaked clay on one bead. Follow the seams with the bark or lightly press the texture of the bark into a smooth area of the unbaked clay. Set this bead aside.

**14** Grind turquoise clay in the food processor as if you were making turquoise beads. However, rather than consolidating the turquoise polymer, bake a handful of the individual nuggets in a preheated oven for 20 minutes. Remove and let cool. These prebaked nuggets work well pressed into amber and coral.

**15** On a second bead, press a baked turquoise nugget or two into the polymer at the intersection of a pair of folds. Let the nugget protrude a bit above the amber's surface (you'll sand it flush with the bead later). Set this bead aside.

**Note:** *True amber beads often have many pits and irregularities on the surface. This is true particularly of amber from the Himalayan region. Pitch was used to fill in the irregularities, and turquoise, coral, or glass substitutes were pushed into the pitch to decorate the bead further. What you are re-creating in this step is the repair and decoration of amber beads.*

**16** Select another bead. Using 100- or 80-grit sandpaper, gently press areas of the sandpaper texture on the bead. Try rolling one corner of the bead over the sandpaper, or press a flatter bead between two pieces of sandpaper. Try embossing a coarse seam across the polymer with a folded edge of sandpaper. Set the bead aside.

**17** Lay the unbaked beads on a nest of polyfill. Bake for 20 minutes in a preheated oven. Do not remove the amber beads from the oven yet.

**18** Turn the oven off after 20 minutes. Leave the beads in the oven and let the oven and beads cool slowly to room temperature. When hot polymer clay hits room temperature air, the surface of the polymer immediately chills, but the interior is still at 275°F. The contrast between the surface and internal temperatures shocks the polymer and opens up microfractures on the surface. These do not fuse together when the clay cools, although they close up. These fractures are usually invisible unless the clay body is primarily translucent or when paint is rubbed on the surface. In that case, these microfractures show up as dark dashes or hyphens. Amber is most likely to set this sequence of events in place, but it is not part of the amber plan. Nothing resembling those dashes occurs in nature, so let the beads cool slowly. When all is cool, remove the polyfill and amber beads from the oven. After removing the beads, turn the oven back on to preheat it so you can set the paint on the beads before buffing.

**19** Under water, sand the beads with 400-, then 600-grit wet-or-dry sandpaper. Go over them once more with either 800- or 1000-grit.

**20** Rub burnt umber paint into all the crevices, folds, nooks, crannies, and other textures, as well as over the surfaces of the beads. Wipe the excess off the surfaces with a slightly damp paper towel. Adjust the tinting on the beads to your desires. Experiment by leaving more paint on some beads. Return the painted beads to the oven for 10 minutes to set the paint. Let them cool in the oven and remove them.

**21** Use 1500-grit wet-or-dry sandpaper to gently sand each bead once more under water. This very fine sanding will allow

This close-up shows the effects of the finishing techniques.

you to quickly polish the surface to a sumptuously high gloss. A high polish shows off the translucent streaks and swirling subtle colors of years of handling.

**22** Polish the beads. Wear latex gloves or mount the bead on a fat knitting needle tightly enough so the bead does not spin around while you're polishing. Be careful not to hold tightly where you have just polished because the friction-warmed clay will be embossed by your fingerprints.

**23** Arrange the amber beads on a 26" length of black rubber cord in a sequence you like. Do not include the two smallest tubular beads. Center the beads on the cord. Knot the cord just above the upper right and upper left beads so they stay centered on the cord.

**24** Put a drop of Zap-a-Gap on one end of the cord. Slip one of the tubular beads over the glue to conceal the end of the cord. Let the glue set up. Repeat on the other end. Congratulations!

# imitating ivory

Imitative ivory is beautiful on its own or in combination with other materials. Coral, turquoise, and lapis add excitement to this tusk-shaped pendant.

## new techniques

hyperfine layering

antiquing using slashing and acrylic paint

embossing

prebaked inlays (page 118)

wire eye pins for stringing (page 118)

Ivory's mellow butteriness soothes and entrances. That sensual surface and air of preciousness make it an obvious material to re-create. Imitating ivory is technically useful as well, suggesting new approaches to polymer clay.

Mixing the color is straightforward: there are minor variations in warmer and cooler off-white tones that you can develop in the clay body. But notice the slight translucency—true ivory is not quite an opaque material, and the thinner the piece the more obvious this is. Additionally, there's the graining, actually a cross-graining that is established as the fibers of the elephant's tusk grow and interweave into a strong, hollow, sturdy structure.

You can't re-create the three-dimensional graining of a true piece of ivory, but if you can simplify it to two-dimensional graining, it's similar to making stripes. Extremely thin stripes. But of what?

And how to integrate that slight translucency? It's really a luminosity, typical of most organically produced materials that incorporate a lot of water in their tissues. If you make ivory without adding some translucency to the clay body, it will look like wood. Luminosity is important for the visual impact of the re-creation.

However if you mix translucent clay directly into the clay body, it may pebble or get too translucent: and the piece will look more like stone than an organic material.

You can integrate translucency and graining together by using a translucent clay and layering it with the ivory-colored clay body rather than mixing it in. If done in fine enough layers, this adds a sense of depth and luminosity to the re-creation, and a subtle graining.

Ivory is easy to work and many approaches to the surface will work. Once baked, the finishing techniques of antiquing and polishing will heighten the imitative ivory's beauty.

**Note:** *Even more than the other imitatives, complete all the steps of ivory before you judge how successful your piece is. The translucent will not be fully translucent until after baking, for instance. Probably all the ivory you've ever seen was polished, so also do that step before judging.*

Ivory was the first imitative I perfected, and is close to my heart. I do not wear real ivory. This imitative is so beautiful, though, that I am delighted to be able to re-create anything I want and to work with it in ways that simulate and then improvise on traditional ivory forms.

A student was returning from a trip abroad wearing her imitative ivory pendant and was stopped by customs for importing banned materials. She had to bend the pendant to prove to them it wasn't real ivory. This can be a very successful technique. Have fun!

# *ivory heart brooch*

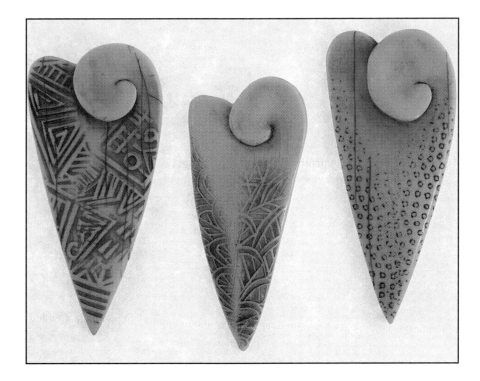

Hearts in community. The project heart pin is on the far right, accompanied by two others with differing surface patterns.

## for this introductory project, you will need:

Fimo Soft
    1/2 ounce white (#0)
    1/2 ounce sahara (#70)
    1/8 ounce golden yellow (#16)
Fimo Classic
    1 ounce Art Translucent (#00)
acrylic paint: burnt umber

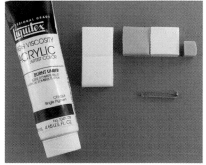

The materials you'll need to make an ivory heart-shaped brooch: polymer clays, paint, a pin back, and glue.

**Note:** *Detailed information on basic polymer clay techniques can be found in Chapter 4, Foundation Processes.*

## instructions

*1* Condition the Art Translucent thoroughly and set it aside.

*2* Mix together the white, sahara, and golden yellow into a solid color.

*3* Roll equal size snakes of each color.

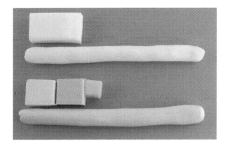

**4** Cut the snakes in half. Roll each half out a little longer and thinner, giving you four thinner snakes. Stack them together in a log that alternates ivory/translucent/ivory/translucent when you look along its sides.

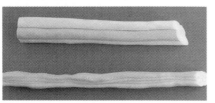

The stripes along the side are your gauge for creating the grain of ivory.

**note**

*Although the checkerboard pattern at the end is eye-catching and looks like millefiore caning, ivory is not a caning technique. The end view of the ivory stock is only important and controllable in the first few stages of construction. Don't judge the ivory stock by looking at the ends for patterns or you'll be irritated later when the ends don't look like anything at all.*

**5** Consolidate this bundle by squeezing it together and pulling it out into a longer striped snake. Don't twist the bundle. Straighten out any swirls and ripples in the graining as you do this. It is very important to maintain a straight grain throughout the construction of this stock.

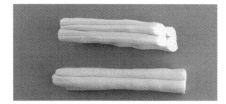

**6** Cut the consolidated snake in half, and half again, making four short snakes. Stack the four short snakes back together as you did above. As much as possible, maintain the alternation of ivory/translucent/ivory/translucent around the circumference of the snake.

**7** Gently squeeze and consolidate the stack into a bundle. Again, be very careful not to twist the snakes. Pull the bundle out again into a longer and more finely striped snake.

**8** Do a third repetition of cutting, stacking, and consolidating the ivory-colored and translucent polymer snakes. Quarter the snake, as above. Stack the four pieces together and bundle them into a solid snake. As you repeat these steps you'll see the ivory and translucent stripes on the sides of the snake getting finer and finer. Repeat this sequence of cutting, stacking, bundling, and pulling out until you can barely perceive a difference between the ivory and translucent stripes.

**9** Although it's hard to see in the photographs, four to six repetitions seem to achieve the right fineness of grain. There is no predetermined number of steps because everyone's techniques and materials are unique. When you think you're getting close, cut a short section off the snake and bake it. The fineness of the lines shows up much more after baking, when the contrast between the pure translucent and the opaque ivory clays is visible. Unbaked translucent clay looks white and the ivory-colored polymer clay itself is half-white, so fine lines next to each other are very hard to distinguish. Avoid going one step too far. This will mix the translucent and ivory clay bodies together in a very labor-intensive way.

**10** Cut the final snake in half and lay the halves next to each other. Press them together to make a wide, flat pad. Smooth and consolidate the pad, creating a section of ivory stock about 1/4" thick.

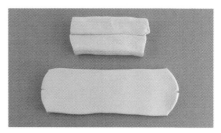

**11** Using the pads of your fingers, gently flatten the stock until it is between 1/8" and 1/4" thick. Never stroke across the grain with your fingers or you will blend the ivory and translucent lines together, eradicating the grain. Roll along the length of the grain with a glass to smooth off the fingerprints. Maintain the straight even grain you have created. All your work so far has been to develop this fine striping in the flat stock. This grain is sensitive to being distorted until you bake the piece.

**12** Use the heart template on page 141 or create your own. Lay the paper pattern on the ivory stock, along the length of the grain. Cut the heart out. Be careful not to bend or skew the grain as you are doing this.

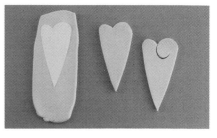

**13** Cut the curl on the right side of the heart by simply continuing the curving line of the right lobe around into the heart-shape. Use an X-acto knife and cut straight down. Gently separate the curl from the clay of the heart shape.

**14** Gently flatten and enlarge the curl a bit by pinching it between your thumb and forefinger. Just a little pinching goes a long way. Overlap the now enlarged (ah, love) curled area back over its original spot, as shown in the photo.

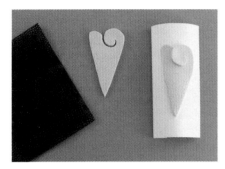

**15** Emboss a pattern on the lower sides of the heart. I used dragon skin to imprint tiny circles into the clay. These show up when paint is rubbed into them after baking.

**16** Create a paper baking armature by curving a piece of card stock into an arch.

**17** Curve the heart by laying it lengthwise on your finger and coaxing the sides down. The curve can be quite shallow and still be effective. Any degree of arch will show up and add to the organic feel of imitative ivory (ivory grows as a cylindrical tusk).

**18** Lay the heart on the paper baking armature. The heart will slump slightly against the armature during baking, but will maintain its delicate curve. Bake in a preheated oven for 20 minutes. Remove and let cool.

**19** Check the position of the elevated curl. If it's loose, use Zap-a-Gap to glue it in place. Don't get glue elsewhere on the surface, as acrylic paint will not adhere to the dried glue and will leave pale spots on the finished piece.

**20** Under water, sand the baked heart with 400-grit, then 600-grit wet-or-dry sandpaper. You may notice the pale dust of sanded polymer filling up the embossed circles. You may rinse it off or use an old soft toothbrush to wash it out.

**21** Add a few (here three) randomly placed slashes to trap the paint and mimic the long cracks in older, dried out ivory. To do this, hold an X-acto knife at a shallow angle to the baked clay's surface and make a single shallow cut. Don't go deeper than one third of the clay's thickness. Be sure to angle the blade, don't cut straight down.

**22** Rub burnt umber acrylic paint all over the heart. Make sure you get paint in the deeper areas like the crease next to the elevated curl. I used my fingers to rub paint on the surface itself, then an old toothbrush to poke paint into deeper areas. Missed spots will show up as white at the end of this process and look very artificial.

**23** Use a slightly damp paper towel to wipe off excess paint. Keep the towel on the dry side or you'll rinse too much paint off and have to start again.

**24** When the degree of tinting suits you, return the piece to the oven for 10 minutes to set the acrylic paint on the polymer clay. Use the baking armature whenever you reheat the piece to maintain its curvature. Remove and let cool.

**25** Sand with 900- or 1000-grit sandpaper very lightly to bring up the natural color of the ivory heart in highlighted areas. Then sand with 1500-grit if available. It will feel as if you are barely affecting the surface, but will speed the buffing and give you a beautiful shine.

**26** Glue the pin back on the back of the piece with Zap-a-Gap. Let the glue dry.

**27** Polish the surface. Buff the margins of the piece as well as the top. Use the pin back to hold the piece. Never put your fingers where you just buffed. For a few seconds after polishing, the polymer is warm from the friction and the piece will be embossed by whatever is pressed tightly against it (like your fingertips).

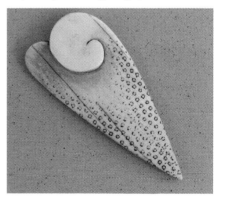

**28** That's it! Very nice. Let the piece cool down for a minute, then pin it on.

# imitating
## agate

Greek and Roman women prized agate jewelry for its elaborate patterning. You can create treasures yourself that are worthy of an Empress.

## new techniques

painting and layering thin polymer clay sheets

thinking three-dimensionally about a block of polymer clay

forming vessels on rocks

piecing slabs

using a belt sander

Agate is a broad category, mineralogically speaking. Agates have been used for adornments for thousands of years. Characterized by alternating fine layers of translucent and opaque stone, sometimes in parallel planes, sometimes in curves, arcs, circles, lacy elaborations of forms, agate's intricate beauty has always fascinated us. How does it know to do that? And more importantly, how can we make polymer do that?

Although it can occur in a rainbow of tints, agate often comes in a narrow color palette, typically browns, black, greys, and cream. You will use that here. Agate's opacity variations can be captured by the polymer's own ability to be both translucent and opaque. Look at a piece of banded agate: some thicknesses of layers repeat and others are unique. This combination of thin repeating and thicker unique layers ensure the realism of your imitations. Too much repetition will look artificial.

How can you re-create those really fine layers? Polymer can be stretched extremely thin, but some layers in agates are even thinner. Visually, the hyperfine opaque layering divides the translucent layers. It allows you to realize you are looking into the agate, across planes of color. To achieve this, you will use acrylic paint, applied directly on unbaked clay. The paint then lays down those very fine opaque layers you want. Acrylic paints, being

polymer themselves, are completely compatible with polymer clay. The paint can be baked, which will fuse it securely to the polymer clay.

By constructing a random collection of thick and thin, opaque and translucent layers, you'll have a block of material you can manipulate for different natural effects. You can cut and reassemble this block, and if you are careful not to distort the clay in ways that solid rock would not distort, almost any reassembly will look like some kind of stone.

Surface and patina are straightforward here. Agates are usually simple, smooth shapes with a satin or high polish, to show off the banding in the stone. Imitative agate can be a magical re-creation. The translucency shows up after baking, sanding, and polishing–changing the piece from interesting to amazing. As always, do not judge until you are done with all the steps.

Once you have the basic concept down, experiment with more color in both the opaque and translucent layers. Look at real agate for comparison and personalize your work from your own experience. You'll have a great time with this imitative technique.

Incidentally, imitative agates grew out of other nonimitative work I was evolving with translucent polymer clays and acrylic paints. Playing around with the possibilities in the polymer/acrylic paint marriage led to a number of new, wonderful approaches to polymer clay art. The point here is that when something interests you, pursue as many aspects of that thing as you can imagine. Let your delight in the "new" lead you.

# banded agate dish

Prēmo
   4 ounces translucent with
   bleach (#5310)
   1 ounce white (#5001)
   1 ounce black  (#5042)
Fimo
   1 ounce black  (#9)
   1/2 ounce cocoa brown (#77)
   1/4 ounce caramel/ochre (#7)
acrylic paint: opaque white and
   raw sienna
nicely shaped rock or a light bulb

The materials you'll need to make
the agate dish: polymer clays and
acrylic paints. You can use either a
rock or a light bulb as an armature
on which to form and bake the
polymer clay dish.

**Note:** *Detailed information on
basic polymer clay techniques can
be found in Chapter 4, Foundation
Processes.*

## instructions

*1* Condition the Prēmo translucent well and set it aside.

*2* Condition one ounce of
white Prēmo with 1/8
ounce ochre Fimo. The result
should be off-white/ivory. Set this
aside.

*3* Condition 1/2 ounce black
Prēmo with 1/2 ounce
brown Fimo and 1/8 ounce ochre
Fimo. The result should be dark
brown. Set this aside.

*4* Mix one ounce black Fimo
with 1/2 ounce black
Prēmo. Set this aside.

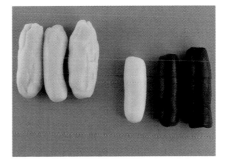

**5** Use a pasta machine to make 2" x 3" sections of translucent polymer as listed below. If the clay sticks to the rollers, sandwich it between sheets of waxed paper or roll it one step thicker, then stretch it thinner by hand.
- 4 sections at #7 (thinnest) setting
- 6 sections at #6 setting
- 3 sections at #2 setting
- 1 section about 1/4" thick (use a glass to roll it flat)

**6** Use a pasta machine to create thin 2" x 3" sections of colored polymer as listed below.
- 2 sections ivory at #5 setting
- 2 sections brown at #6 setting
- 1 section brown at #3 setting
- 2 sections black at #7 setting
- 3 sections black at #5 setting
- 1 section black about 1/4" thick (roll with a glass)

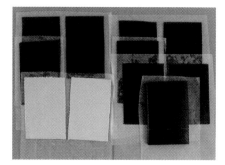

**7** Mix the white and raw sienna acrylic paints to make off-white. Paint one side of all the translucent sections and paint one side of the thickest black piece. Use a wide, soft brush and stroke the paint on evenly. Add as little water as necessary to paint fluidly. The paint should be thick and smooth.

**Note:** *Use these painted sections within a day or two. Unbaked painted clay will stiffen after this time. If the painted clay layers crack apart as you laminate them onto other clays, they are too old.*

**8** When the paint is dry, stack the layers in the order below (painted side up unless otherwise indicated). Align the edges precisely when stacking to eliminate waste to trim off later. Smooth each layer as you stack it to ease out any air bubbles trapped between the layers. Avoid pulling or stretching the painted layers since this will thin or fracture the paint. The paint mimics the fine layers of opaque minerals in the stone and should remain solid and thick on the clay.
- 1 layer 1/4" translucent
- 4 layers #7 painted translucent
- 1 layer #5 black
- 1 layer #6 painted translucent, *painted side down*
- 1 layer #5 ivory
- 1 layer #2 painted translucent
- 1 layer #6 painted translucent
- 1 layer #7 black
- 1 layer #6 painted translucent, *painted side down*
- 1 layer #7 black
- 1 layer #2 painted translucent, *painted side down*
- 1 layer #6 brown
- 1 layer #6 painted translucent
- 1 layer #3 brown
- 1 layer #5 black
- 1 layer #6 painted translucent
- 1 layer #5 black
- 1 layer #5 ivory
- 1 layer #2 painted translucent
- 1 layer #6 brown

- 1 layer 1/4" black, *painted side down*

You should end up with 24 sections laid on top of each other. If your layers are different, don't worry. The impact of the agate comes from a variety of different and contrasting thicknesses and opacities. Just vary the layers and the agate will look fine.

**9** Firmly press the layers together. Pick up the block of layers in your hands and press from both sides, evenly compressing the layers of polymer. Consolidate the clays and paints together until they feel like a solid block of material. This step is important: it will minimize the tendency of the baked layers to delaminate under the stress of later sanding.

**10** Slice off a segment of the block at an angle. Notice that an angled cut across the block shows the increasing depth of the translucent clay, wedging back through the painted layers. All slices used in making agate objects should be cut at an angle so the planes of thin and thick, translucent and opaque, have the most depth.

**11** Make a small circle of the remaining dark brown clay and set it on the rock (or light bulb). Although this is the top of the rock, it will be the bottom of the bowl, so the finished bowl will rest on this spot. Slabs of layered clay will extend from this circle in an organic manner, replicating the faulted banding of true agate.

**12** Slice a slab from the block about 3/8" thick. Remember to cut it at an angle. Every slab from this block will have a black end and a translucent end. Taper the slab's shape toward the black end so the sides are wider at the translucent end and narrower at the black end. Since you are going to add several slices around the contour of the rock, you'll need to shape the clay sections to accommodate this bowl shape.

**13** Butt the narrower black end of this section against the dark brown central circle on the rock. Press the clay against the rock. Push the clay together thoroughly so the slabs feel fused together. Always press the clay in the same direction so the angle of the layers is maintained during your manipulation. The direction you push should reinforce the angle. Don't worry about the smearing of the clay layers that occurs on the outside of the bowl. The outer surface will be heavily sanded later to reveal the perfect layering.

**14** Think about the edge of the slabs–where each slab will meet with its neighbor. These obviously cannot be sanded but do need to be securely pressed together for the slabs to adhere. Place the slab in its selected spot and check the fit. Trim as needed for that spot. Make sure the matching section also has a clean edge. Always trim the edges of each slab as you apply it to the rock and against its neighbor. As long as you press two clean edges together, and the contact plane that connects them is straight, the distortion on the surface that results from pushing the clay around will not affect the interior clean contact plane. You will sand the surface messiness off later.

**15** Continue fitting, tapering, and adding layers. The photo shows two slabs on the rock and a third one being measured for fit. Depending on the shape of the rock, the degree of tapering may vary quite a bit. Nature varies much more, so don't worry about it, just concentrate on keeping the edges of the slabs straight and clean.

Don't be concerned about the irregular upper edge that the slabs

make on the rock. You will trim this later. Unless you are working on a perfect sphere, the upper edge will be uneven. The uneven edge will actually create a more interesting and natural looking bowl when finished.

**16** Cover the entire upper section of the rock with the tapered and joined slabs. Don't add clay any higher than the widest part of the rock, or you won't be able to get the rock out after baking.

**17** Turn the rock over and press gently to establish a flat spot on the bottom (the base of the bowl).

**18** Trim the upper edge of the bowl. Cut straight across the slabs. To avoid distorting the soft polymer, roll the tissue blade against the rock rather than stroking with the blade.

**19** Preheat the oven and bake the polymer clay and rock for 30 minutes. Remove and let the dish and rock cool to room temperature. This will take some time because the rock will hold the heat.

**20** When the dish and rock are cool, remove the baked polymer from the rock. If you do this before the clay has cooled, you risk separating the joints between the slabs. When polymer clay is hot, it is fragile, no matter how well polymerized it may be. If a joint does break, let everything cool down, and glue the joint with Zap-a-Gap. After sanding, the repair will be invisible.

**21** Time for the belt sander. Be gentle. Sand the outside of the dish with the sander, gently refining the outer surface until it is smooth and an attractive shape. Sand until the edges of the painted layers are crisp and sharp and all the smears of clay have been removed. Maintain a precise flat upper edge to the dish.

**22** Sand the outside of the dish by hand with 600-and 900-grit wet-or-dry sandpaper, under water. This will make it quick and easy to polish the dish to a beautiful shine.

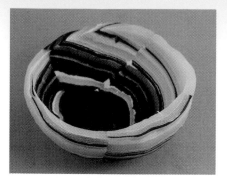

**23** Sand the inside of the dish. If you have a Dremel or other adaptable motorized tool, this is an excellent place to use it. If not, sand by hand. Start with 240-grit, then 320-, then 400-grit. Again, remove any visible smearing and work into the surface until the edges of the painted layers are crisp and sharp.

**24** Polish the outside of the dish and the upper edge. Options for the inside of the dish include leaving it as is, using a lacquer on the surface to give a semi-gloss shine, or if you have a Dremel, using the small buffer to shine it up. (I used Golden semi-gloss varnish on the inside.)

**25** Congratulate yourself on what a wonderful object you made. It's beautiful!

# imitating metals

Imitating metals can run the gamut from realistic "silver" bead caps to rusted elements, to smooth golden areas, and on into iridescent and metallic surfaces that refer to metals, beetle wings, aluminum airplane skins, or ancient imperial jewelry. The basic principles are simple but the ultimate result can be quite expressive.

Color on most metals is a combination of actual color and reflected color. If you close one eye, you can see this clearly. The surface of the object reads as metal because of highlights and mirrored colors from things nearby. In imitating this effect, the color exists in combination with its luster or reflectiveness. This strong degree of shininess is more pronounced than the metallic effects available in even the most metallic of polymer clay bodies.

So instead you will rely on surface paints to provide this metallic shine. The underlying clay will be completely covered by careful applications of paint. However, you will still use corresponding clay body colors in case an area becomes exposed. No one paint is lustrous enough to convey the richness of true metal. You will mix a blend of metallic paints and metallic powders to approach the complexity of silver, gold, and other metals. Since metals are opaque, the clay body mix is straightforward.

Surface characteristics create the reflectivity of true metals. The reason you see those reflections is that light is being bounced off different surface textures, like areas on decorative castings or filigree work, or from irregularities in the surface from pitting, corrosion, and oxidation. To accentuate this contrast, you will enhance the highlights as well as the darker colors in deeper areas.

More than the other materials mimicked in this book, the surfaces of metals are strong indicators of age and handling. Agate, for instance, varies very little over time. Metal objects are rigid materials that then wear away. So marks made before baking with hard objects or after baking once the clay itself is hard, are most likely to create a metal-like surface texture.

Get a piece of metal and examine it. Observe the fine-scale texturing on a nice pair of silver earrings and how much light and dark contrast there is between the highest areas and the lowest.

The patina on metal imitations is straightforward because the surface, at least in the higher areas, needs to be glossy to reflect those highlights. On some of your pieces, you may simulate antiquing—the applied patina of oxidation, typically black or dark gray on silver and blue-green on brass, bronze, and copper. Gold, the incorruptible, does not tarnish. I use a very slightly darkened version of the gold paint to aid in defining lower areas.

A final note about imitating metals: Metals can require more attention to the surface painting than other imitatives. The bulk of their success lies in this painting, so allow yourself to experiment, play, adjust, until you have a feel for your unique way of handling the painting. Observe your own process as you go. Ultimately, all learning is self-taught. And have fun with this!

Both on their own and in combination with other materials, imitative metals will add sophistication and richness, and naturally enhance your work.

## new techniques

creating an embossing plate for a specific piece

mixing complex metallic paints and powder blends

antiquing metals

fitting picture frames

making a frame hanger

# *silver spirals picture frame*

## for this introductory project, you will need:

Fimo: 2 ounces white (#02)
powders: Fimo silver metallic,
  PearlEx silver metallic
acrylic paints: black, burnt umber,
  silver (2 brands)
3" length of 18-gauge silver-color
  wire
texturing surface or carved
  embossing plate

The materials for making the silver picture frame: white polymer clay, metallic powders, black, silver, and burnt umber acrylic paints, and silver wire (for the hanger).

**Note:** *Detailed information on basic polymer clay techniques can be found in Chapter 4, Foundation Processes.*

## instructions

*1* Thoroughly condition the white clay.

*2* Make three flat pads roughly 3" by 4" and about earlobe thickness. Roll these smooth with a glass.

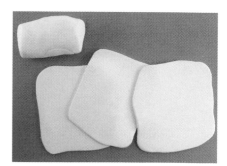

*3* Cut out the frame templates on page 142 or use your own. There are three template pieces: the front, the interior layer (provides the shallow space to accommodate a photo), and the back. Set aside the frame front pattern and one of the pads of clay.

*4* Lay the patterns for the interior and back on the remaining pads of clay. Roll across them gently with a glass to adhere the paper to the polymer.

*5* Cut out the shapes of the interior and back layers. Don't remove the paper patterns from the clay. You will bake the polymer pieces with the patterns on them to stabilize the shapes and avoid distortion of the pieces when you move them to the oven.

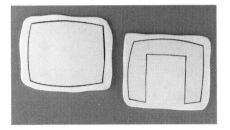

*6* Bake these two pieces in a preheated oven for 30 minutes. Remove and let cool.

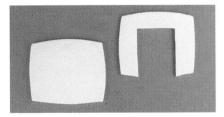

*7* Mix together about 1/4 teaspoon each of the two silver powders. Any time you are working with powders, wear a dust mask. This light silver powder will be the mold release for embossing a pattern into the clay.

*8* Coat one surface of the remaining white clay pad thoroughly with the silver powder mixture.

*9* Select a flat mold with a sharply incised pattern. For this project, I baked a plain polymer plate about 1/4" by 4" by 6". Then I carved a random pattern of spirals into the clay with a small, v-shaped linoleum carving blade. The crisp, raised lines produced by this blade nicely mimic the sharp angularity of a true metal surface.

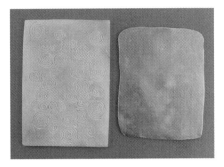

*10* Place the clay pad, powder side up, on a piece of paper. Roll over it to adhere the polymer pad to the paper. This will stabilize the frame shape you are about to make. Set the carved plate on the polymer. Roll firmly once over the unbaked polymer with a glass or press down firmly with your hand, embossing the spirals deeply on the unbaked polymer. Lift the mold up and examine the surface. If not satisfied, mix the polymer clay thoroughly, roll it out in a pad, and try again. You are not wasting the clay or the effort–you are learning. Don't settle for less than just the way you want it.

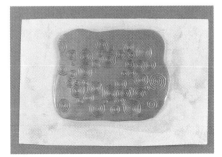

*11* Select your favorite area of the embossed surface, bearing

in mind that the central section will be removed for the window. Place the frame front template on the embossed polymer and cut out the frame front. Take care not to distort the clay as you cut.

*12* Use the underlying paper to transfer the frame to the oven. Bake in a preheated oven for 30 minutes. Remove and cool, then peel the baked frame off the paper.

*13* Check the fit of the three pieces by stacking them together as if the frame was finished. If any edges stick out, trim with an X-acto knife or belt sander.

*14* Mix about 1/2 teaspoon each of the black, burnt umber, and silver acrylic paints to create a dark neutral metallic paint. If possible, refer to a piece of silver or other metal to re-create the actual color. Use a stiff brush or a sponge brush to push this dark paint into the deepest areas of the embossed relief.

*15* Pat the surface with your hand or a paper towel to remove the paint from the higher sections of the relief. Brush the side of your hand across the highest points to remove all the paint from them. Continue until the paint blends from the darkest in the deep areas to no paint at all on the top of the embossing. Paint the edges and the inner margin of the frame.

**16** When you are satisfied with the paint, put the piece back in the oven for 10 minutes to set the acrylic paint on the surface.

**17** Position and glue the interior layer to the back layer. Make sure the inside corners (where the photo will rest) are glued continuously along the inside edge to prevent the corners of the photo from slipping between the two layers.

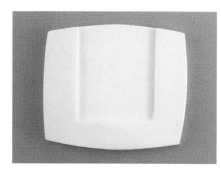

**18** Make a wire hanger by cutting a 3" length of wire and bending it in a horseshoe shape. Use round-nose pliers to curl the ends of the wire. On a cement surface outdoors (bricks break, wood is too soft), hammer the curled ends of the wire flat. These curls will give you a larger surface area for gluing.

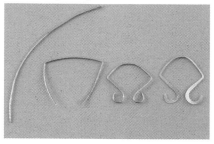

**19** Glue the flattened sections of the wire hanger to the upper center of the frame back. After the glue is completely dry, gently bend the upper arc of the hanger slightly away from the frame back for ease of hanging.

**20** Glue the frame front to the interior layer. As before, be sure to get the glue right up to the edge of the interior frame to avoid gaps. Press securely together. Let the glue dry.

**21** Brush or sponge the dark metallic paint on the back of the frame. For a bit of texture on the finished surface, bounce a stiff brush in the paint while it is still wet. Brush or sponge the edges of the completed frame, using the texture of the paint to obscure the seams between the layers.

**22** Mix a small amount of a light silver paint. Put on a dust mask. Mix in a bit of silver powder. This will give you a very metallic light silver paint.

**23** Dab your finger in this paint. Lightly brush across the dark paint on the back of the frame, moving your finger in one direction only. Your finger is mimicking the light, slanting across the surface textures. Practice on the back to get the feel of this gesture before doing the same on the front, highlighting the raised spirals. Allow the paint to touch any larger open areas in the design as well. Again, refer to an actual metal object for the appearance of the paint. When I did this, I found that there was much more contrast between higher and deeper areas than I'd expected.

**24** Touch up the edges of the frame. Set the piece aside for a few hours to let the paint dry. Never put a piece back in the oven after applying Zap-a-Gap, since the heat deteriorates the glue.

**25** Slide in a photo and hang the frame.

# imitating faience

Have you seen that charming Egyptian hippopotamus sculpture, small and blue, with lotus flowers painted on his sides? He's made of faience. Faience, the classic luscious blue material, is a fused glass powder that creates its own glaze as minerals in the powder come to the surface during firing. Most commonly associated with ancient Egypt, faience is also produced in other parts of the world, notably China and Central Asia. Despite its age, much of it is preserved in near-perfect condition, and the precise, delicate workmanship is inspiring.

Imitative faience introduces a new element into your toolbox—the use of a liquid material over the surface, similar to a glaze in ceramics. True faience is self-glazing. You will mimic this in a two-stage process: baking an underlying form, then applying a tinted Liquid Sculpey as a glaze, and rebaking.

First, go back to the basics of color, translucency, surface, and patina. Faience is most recognizable as a clean turquoise blue, but was manufactured in many colors such as yellows, reds, whites, and greens. On some pieces, oxidation over time altered those colors even further. The faience you will re-create is the classic blue material, unoxidized.

So you'll mix a blue clay body and use a blue tint in the TLS. The success of your faience will stem from controlling opacity and translucency in these two components. The depth of the tinted translucent glaze will be most apparent over an opaque blue clay body, as it fills in the recessed areas.

The surface characteristics of faience are usually this translucent

To ancient Egyptians, faience was more than a substitute for turquoise, it was a sacred material in its own right.

glazed effect, with a semi-glossy to glossy shine. For mimicking that glassy surface on the originals, you'll use a glossy lacquer in place of the normal polish finish. TLS is so resilient that sanding and buffing do not work well.

The faience bowl project echoes a classic ancient Egyptian design, a small bowl with feet. Adding the feet in a second baking, before the TLS glaze, adds information about multiple baking to your toolbox: baking part of a form to make it rigid, then adding on new elements and rebaking. This will be a necessary tool for creating larger, more complex three-dimensional forms.

Once you understand the information here, experiment with different color combinations of clay bodies and glazes. Working with TLS can be exciting and provocative, creatively speaking.

## new techniques

multiple baking

figurative modeling for feet

tinting Translucent Liquid Sculpey

glazed effects with Translucent Liquid Sculpey

# *footed faience bowl*

## for this introductory project, you will need:

Fimo Classic
    1-1/2 ounces light turquoise
    (#32)
    1/2 ounce blue (#37)
    1/2 ounce white (#0)
Translucent Liquid Sculpey
acrylic paint: translucent ultrama-
    rine
gloss varnish

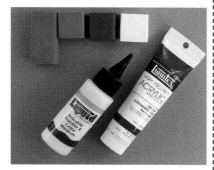

The materials for making a footed blue faience bowl: polymer clays, Translucent Liquid Sculpey, and transparent blue acrylic paint. The bowl is formed on a light bulb.

**Note:** *Detailed information on basic polymer clay techniques can be found in Chapter 4, Foundation Processes.*

## instructions

*1* Mix all the polymer clays together into a medium bright blue. Set a walnut-sized piece of this clay aside for later use.

*2* Roll the remaining clay into a ball with no folds or seams and flatten this into a circle about 1/4" thick.

**3** Center a light bulb, standing straight up, on the circle of clay. Press the bulb down slightly to emboss a flat spot for the base of the bowl. The more centered and vertical the bulb, the better. You will bake the bowl on the light bulb.

**4** Ease the clay up on the side of the bulb, keeping it as even in thickness as possible.

**5** Trim the clay's edge to an even height on the sides of the bulb. Don't go higher than the widest point of the bulb or you won't be able to remove the bulb after baking. One easy way to trim the edge straight is to stand the bowl/light bulb up. Hold a stiff card against the bowl and mark the lowest point of the bowl on the card. Rotate the bowl, holding the card against the bowl, mark that lowest point all the way around the bowl, and join those points into a line. Trim to that line.

**6** Roll a glass along the upper edge of the clay, pressing it into a tapered shape as shown. Lean the lip of the glass against the light bulb to stabilize it. Modifying the edge adds refinement to the bowl's shape.

**7** Use a knitting needle or other tool to emboss a fluted pattern on the outside of the bowl. Just hold the light bulb and roll the knitting needle over the clay. It's not necessary to pattern the base of the bowl. Stand the bowl/light bulb up in a preheated oven and bake for 30 minutes. Remove and let cool.

**8** Halve the walnut-size ball of clay you set aside earlier and roll into two small balls.

**9** Model each ball into a triangular proto-foot shape and pull a nub up from the smallest point of the triangle. This nub will become the ankle. If you haven't done any modeling before, practice this first. The truth is, these feet will be charming no matter how precisely you make them.

**10** Use an X-acto knife to emboss the lines between the toes. Make four toes (it's easier to split a shape into fourths than fifths).

**11** Press the edge of the X-acto blade against the front of the toes, separating the toe tips. This creates a more realistic, rounded edge to the toe shapes.

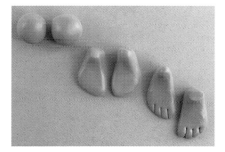

**12** Pull up the ankle nub and trim it to provide a flat upper surface to the ankle. Set the feet on a piece of paper at an angle to each other. These feet must create a stable base under the bowl.

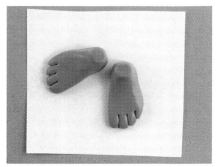

**13** Press the feet down so the polymer adheres to the paper, which will go in the oven under the feet as a tray.

**14** Remove the light bulb from the baked polymer bowl. It should come out easily with a minimal amount of wiggling.

**15** Set the baked bowl on top of the feet. Center the weight of the bowl over the feet so the bowl will stand up. I tilted the front of the bowl down a bit to help balance it.

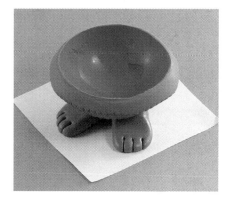

**16** During the baking process, unbaked clay softens further before it hardens. The heaviness of this baked bowl above these soft unbaked feet will topple the whole form if it is not braced during baking. Make a folded triangle or roll of paper and place it securely between the feet. The paper needs to support the weight of the bowl completely. Take care that the paper does not push into the unbaked clay feet and emboss a dent in them during baking.

**17** Bake in a preheated oven for 30 minutes. Remove and let cool.

**18** Time for the Translucent Liquid Sculpey (TLS). As noted in the materials and tools section, TLS is a hyper-plasticized polymer clay. Be prepared–TLS gets everywhere, like mildew. Work on a glass or glazed ceramic surface or dish. Always wear latex gloves to prevent absorbing TLS into your skin. TLS bakes at a higher temperature for less time. Bake TLS outside or in a well-ventilated space, as the fumes are stronger than regular polymer. Despite all these precautions, TLS is worth using: it's a fantastic material, full of potential and ability. Don't avoid it, just respect it.

**19** Preheat the oven to 300°F. Mix two table-spoons of Liquid Sculpey with a very small dab of transparent ultramarine paint. Use a tooth-pick to add small amounts of paint into the TLS. Stir thoroughly and add more ultramarine if necessary. Tinted TLS will be darker and more transparent after baking. Test the glaze color by dabbing the tinted TLS on a scrap of the blue clay and baking for 10 minutes. The color should be rich and dark.

**20** Holding the bowl by the feet, apply a thin even coat of the tinted TLS to the outside and inside of the bowl.

**21** Set the bowl on a piece of paper and bake in the hotter oven for 10 minutes. Remove and let cool.

**22** When the bowl has cooled, add another coat of tinted TLS to the bowl, and one or two coats on the feet. Bake for another 10 minutes, remove, and let cool. Again, this will be easier if you work on a piece of paper that you can transfer to the oven. Don't work on a bare oven tray unless you know you will remember to remove the baked TLS from the tray later. How's the glaze on the bowl? If you'd like it darker, repeat the glazing steps until you are satisfied with the richness of color.

**note**

*Although I have stressed not to bake polymer clays above 280°F to avoid discoloration, Fimo opaque is the one exception. It can tolerate short bursts of this higher temperature.*

**23** Lacquer the glazed areas of the bowl, including the feet, with a gloss varnish. Use two or three coats on the shaped upper edge to accentuate the depth of the surface. If you like, you may try my variation on applying glaze to the inside of bowl. I prefer a satin finish here. When lacquering this area, I wear latex gloves and as soon as I brush the lacquer on, I wipe it around with my finger, as if I am smearing a layer of paint around. The more you manipulate the lacquer, the duller the finish will be. Practice on another piece first.

# chapter 6

# intermediate projects

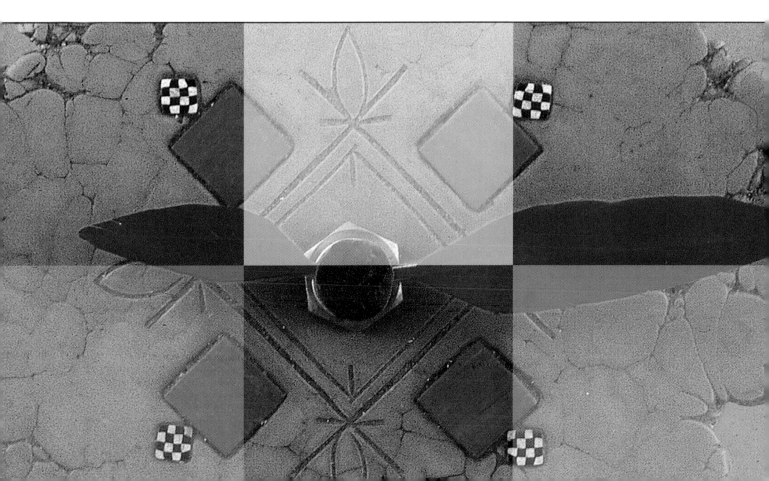

# lapis and ivory accordion book

*1* From the chopped lapis mixture, make two pads by consolidating, flattening, and rolling to earlobe thickness. To ensure the clay grains are sufficiently consolidated, lift the pads up and check the underside. If the pads crumble apart, lay them down and push them together from the sides until the grains are tightly consolidated. Smooth the pads by rolling them with a glass.

*2* Cut a 3" by 4" paper template. Lay this template on the pads of lapis stock and cut two rectangles.

*Note: It's usually easier to make two small well-made pads of lapis than one large one; thus my instructions to make two. However, you can also make one large pad and cut both rectangles from it.*

*3* Bake the two lapis rectangles in a preheated oven for 30 minutes. Remove and let cool.

*4* Sand the baked lapis rectangles under water, as always when using wet-or-dry sandpaper, using 400-, 600-, and 1000-grit sandpaper. To speed up the polishing process, also sand with 1500-grit if you have it. The large flat area of these rectangular covers gives you a good opportunity to check your sanding practice, since they will polish up quickly and evenly if well sanded.

*5* Choose the nicest looking side of each rectangle and buff that side only. The paper accordion will be glued to one side of each rectangle and glue will not stick as well to polished polymer. Set the polished covers aside.

*6* Find a small object to recreate as molded ivory elements for the front of the book. I chose a carved silver Chinese character meaning happiness. Make a mold of the object, using cornstarch as a mold release (refer to page 60 for mold making instructions). Bake the mold and let it cool completely.

*7* Using small sections of the ivory mixture, make two casts from the mold. You may use purchased ivory color clay here if you wish, although for maximum voluptuousness the imitative ivory will be best. The grain of the ivory should go vertically on these elements. Trim any excess polymer from the elements. Bake in a preheated oven for 20 minutes. Remove and cool.

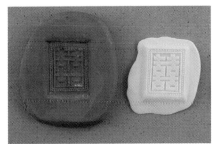

## for this intermediate project, you will need:

- 3 ounces chopped lapis mixture, enough for two 3" by 4" rectangles (see page 77 for lapis instructions)
- 1" segment of ivory stock for small inlays (see page 94 for ivory instructions)
- acrylic paint: burnt umber
- 10" length of 18-gauge gold-colored wire
- paper for pages, enough to create one strip at least 24" by 4"

The basic materials for making a lapis book with ivory embellishments and accordion paper pages. You'll need about three ounces of the lapis clay mixture and a small amount of the ivory clay mixture, burnt umber acrylic paint, gold-colored wire, paper, and glues.

*Note: Detailed information on basic polymer clay techniques can be found in Chapter 4, Foundation Processes.*

**8** Sand the ivory elements with 400-, 600-, then 1000-grit sandpaper and apply burnt umber paint to antique them. Polish to finish them (refer to page 97 for details on finishing ivory).

**9** Center one ivory element on the polished side of each cover. Use Zap-a-Gap to glue them in place.

**10** Using 18-gauge gold-colored wire, design the wire shapes you'd like to frame the ivory elements. Measure the length of wire necessary and add 1/8" on each end of each wire section to bend into a "foot" that can be glued into the baked covers. Cut (be precise) and bend the wire sections in the desired shape.

**11** Mark where the wires will be placed on the covers. Emboss a small dent in the surface of the baked polymer clay by pressing the wire sections down on the covers, as if you were trying to push them into the clay. Make sure you can see the marks.

**12** Drill holes at the marks. Use a drill bit that is slightly smaller than the wire you are using for the frame.

**13** Put a drop of Zap-a-Gap on the tip of each wire foot and slide the feet into the drilled holes. Be consistent with the pattern of overlap of the wire sections. On my covers, the vertical sections were glued in first and the horizontal sections overlap them. Don't use too much glue or smear it around the holes.

**14** Now for the pages of this lovely little book. Make a strip of paper 4" high and 24" long. For a handmade look and a softer edge, tear rather than cut the strip.

Accordion books are made from one long pleated piece of paper. For this book, each page will be 3" wide by 4" high, the same size as the covers. The first page (or section of the pleat) will be glued to the inside of the front cover and the last section will be glued to the inside of the back cover. Since these pages are 3" wide, a 24" strip of paper will make eight pages (24 ÷ 3 = 8), six pages to use plus the two sections glued to the covers. However, you can turn the book over and open up the pages from the other side, so you actually have two six-page books! How wonderful.

**Note:** *I suggest a 24" strip of paper because many attractive art papers come 30" wide, giving you plenty of width for a 24" strip.*

**15** Pleat the paper in an accordion, up and down.

Each section should be 3" wide and 4" high.

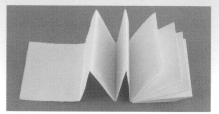

**16** Line up the first section of the accordion with the back of one of the lapis covers. Make sure the pleated strip starts with a valley fold.

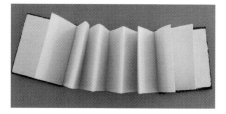

**17** Spread Sobo or other white glue over the entire back side of the front cover. Make sure the glue is smooth on the polymer or it will leave little bumps on the inside covers of the book. Dilute the glue slightly if necessary to make a spreadable consistency.

**18** Glue the first paper section precisely on the inside front cover. The valley fold should fall exactly at the edge of the polymer cover and the entire accordion, when closed, should line up with the edges of the cover. If not, correct it now, while the glue is still a little wet.

**19** Spread glue on the inside back cover. With the accordion closed, gently place the cover on top of the last page, lined up with the edges. Ensure that no glue seeps down and glues the accordion pages together. Press tightly together for 10 minutes or until the glue has started to set up. Let the glue dry completely. Turn it over, open it up, and admire what you made. Excellent!

# inlaid
## turquoise
## clock

## for this intermediate project, you will need:

Fimo Classic
  2 ounces light turquoise (#32)
  1 ounce white (#0)
  1/8 ounce golden yellow (#16)
prebaked inlays
coral sheet (see page 86 for coral
  making instructions)
red sheet
small checkerboard cane (see page
  63 for cane making instructions)
small bit of lapis (see page 77 for
  lapis making instructions)
acrylic paint: raw sienna
fine dust or dirt
clock mechanism with 1/2" shaft
red feather
AA battery

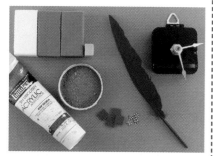

The materials you'll need to make an inlaid turquoise clock: polymer clays, prebaked coral, lapis, and checkerboard cane inlays, raw sienna acrylic paint, a little fine dust or dirt, a clock mechanism, one AA battery for the clock, a red feather, and glue.

**Note:** *Detailed information on basic polymer clay techniques can be found in Chapter 4, Foundation Processes.*

## instructions

*1* Mix the three polymer clays into a well-blended solid turquoise color with no streaks.

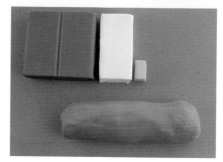

*2* Run this clay through a food processor, chopping it into nuggets.

*3* Push the nuggets together into a thick pancake. Roll this pancake smooth, maintaining a thickness of at least 3/16". Leave the edges untrimmed to mimic the irregular contours of the stone and add visual interest.

*4* Cut a hole in the pancake center to accommodate the clock's shaft. To make a hole this size, I used the cap of a Sharpie marker. I broke off the plastic clip and it became a perfect hole cutter. In a pinch, use what's at hand. Using this center hole as a guide, make four equidistant marks around the middle of the face, like the cardinal numbers on a clock. These will indicate where to place the inlays.

*5* Gather a sheet of prebaked coral inlay and a small prebaked checkerboard cane. You may use a prebaked sheet of a bright orange/red if you don't have a sheet of coral made up. Cut four squares of the coral sheet about 1/4" across and four thin checkerboard slices, about 1/16" square.

*6* Space the four coral squares at each of the cardinal points. Then add the checkerboard sections above each coral square, tilted at 45°. See the photo for guidance or create your own design. Press the inlays into the clay. Roll over the surface of the face with a glass to smooth the clay and remove any fingerprints. The inlays should be flush or just above the surface. You'll be sanding the object later and can sand the inlays flush at that point.

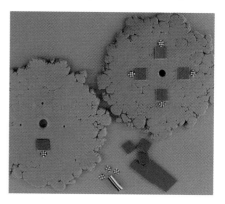

*7* Bake the clock face in a preheated oven for 30 minutes. Remove and let cool.

*8* Hum the mantra of the imitative techniques, "Sand/Carve/Paint/Buff." Under water, sand across the entire clock face with 400-, then 600-grit wet-or-dry sandpaper.

*9* Draw a simple design on the face as a guide for carving.

With a fine, v-shaped linoleum blade, carve the template from page 141 or use one of your own design. (Of course, you may carve a free-hand pattern or skip the carving altogether.)

**10** Rub raw sienna acrylic paint on the surface of the clock face. Rub a bit of dust or fine dirt into the carving and the fine crevices between the original nuggets to add a little age and personality to the surface. Gently wipe excess paint off the surface with a slightly damp paper towel.

**11** Put the clock face back in the oven for 10 minutes to set the paint. Remove and let cool.

**12** Polish the clock face on a buffing wheel. If you want additional shine, first use a 1000-grit or other very fine wet-or-dry sandpaper, which prepares the surface. This will remove some of the paint but the increased sheen compensates. Experiment to find what you like best.

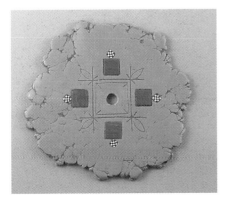

**13** Separate the parts of the clock mechanism, laying the parts out in sequence on your worktable so you can put it back together easily. Notice that the shaft of the mechanism is long enough to go through the clock face and not much farther. The shafts come in different lengths so be aware of what you are purchasing and get one that corresponds to your specific project.

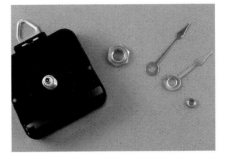

You will add design elements (feathers) on the clock hands. In your designs, always look for ways to make your aesthetic consistent throughout your piece. The feathers will match the intention established by the clock face itself.

**14** Use scissors to cut a red feather into smaller feather shapes that fit on the clock face. Be careful and precise. Feathers are an unusual texture to cut and you may choose to practice first. These feathers are available in many bright colors from a craft store.

**15** Cut narrow strips of red prebaked inlay the same width as the metal hands of the clock. These will serve as an intermediate layer between the feathers and the skinny metal clock hands.

**16** Glue the small feathers on the red baked polymer clay strips with Zap-a-Gap. Let the glue dry completely. Glue these polymer strips on the metal hands, using Zap-a-Gap. Let the glue dry completely.

**17** Assemble the clock components, following the instructions on the package. Add the clock face above the rubber washer and below the brass nut. Be gentle with the feathered hands.

**18** You may cut a small disc of lapis prebaked inlay or a dark blue polymer clay mix and very carefully glue that to the top of the shaft. This final element adds another personal touch. Use Sobo for this particular gluing operation. Although Sobo is not a permanent glue for metal/polymer joints, mistakes with Zap-a-Gap in this part of the clock will seize up the mechanism. There's no stress on this joint, and the Sobo will hold. You may even use a little ball of unbaked clay for this.

**19** Insert the battery and set the time. Hang on the wall. Admire your work!

# inlaid ivory tusk pendant with coral and lapis

# instructions

**1** Refer to page 94 and make some ivory stock. Taper one end of a 1-1/2" by 3/4" diameter ivory section by rolling and gently pinching it with your fingers. You may try pulling slightly to enhance the shape but avoid twisting the ivory grain. Keep the surface as smooth and even as you can while doing the shaping. Smooth any seams by stroking with the grain until the surface is even.

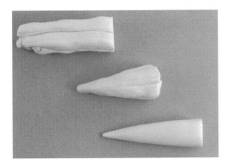

**2** Refine the surface of the cone by rolling the polymer in an arc, which will maintain the conical shape and flatten any surface irregularities at the same time. You are used to rolling snakes by moving your palms up and down parallel to the table but this will never create a cone, just a cylinder. Rolling conical shapes uses a slightly different motion, rolling in an arc, not a plane. Pivot from the base of the palm as if waving; keep your wrist in the same spot and swivel your palm from side to side. This action accentuates the cone and smooths the surface evenly. Practice on scrap clay first if you haven't done this before.

**3** From the library of prebaked inlays you have accumulated, select thin sheets of turquoise, coral, and lapis, or quickly make thin sheets of red, dark blue, and turquoise blue polymer clay. Bake them completely in a preheated oven for 20

minutes. Prebaked inlays must not be underbaked or they will chip and fragment when you cut them up for inlaying.

**4** Gently stroke the tip of the tusk into a slight curve. Do not bend it, persuade it. The curve begins at the tusk's top and becomes most pronounced at the tip.

**5** Use an X-acto knife to cut the prebaked inlay shapes as shown on the tusk or in a design of your own. As you see here, the finishing on the inlays will occur with the finishing—sanding, painting, buffing—of the tusk at the end of this process.

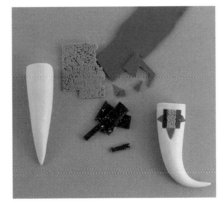

**6** Press the inlays gently into the polymer clay on the face of the ivory. Any slight gap between the inlays and the ivory polymer will fill with paint later in this process, creating a fine dark line around the inlays and adding realism to the effect of the inlaying. If the polymer distorts more than you'd like, carefully press the ivory back into position against the inlays.

**7** Lay the unbaked, inlaid tusk lightly on a bed of polyfill for baking. Unaffected by the oven temperature, this material supports delicate polymer clay shapes dur-

## for this intermediate project, you will need:

imitative ivory, 1-1/2" long by 3/4" diameter (see page 94 for ivory making instructions)
imitative lapis mixture, enough for two 1-1/2" discs (see page 77 for lapis making instructions)
imitative coral bead (see page 86 for coral making instructions)
prebaked coral, turquoise, and lapis inlays
acrylic paint: burnt umber
6" length of 12- or 14-gauge silver or nickel silver wire
36" length of black rubber cording

The materials needed to make a pendant necklace of an inlaid ivory tusk with lapis and coral: premade ivory stock, prebaked inlays of turquoise, lapis, and coral, burnt umber paint, silver wire, and black rubber cord.

**Note:** *Detailed information on basic polymer clay techniques can be found in Chapter 4, Foundation Processes.*

ing baking, when the clay gets soft and slumps. If you were to bake this tusk directly on the tray of the oven, it would have a flat spot on the back (very untusklike).

**8** Bake in a preheated oven for 30 minutes. Remove and let cool.

**9** Finish by sanding, painting, and buffing as for all imitative techniques. Before painting, make sure the top of the tusk, where the lapis and coral beads will sit, is completely flat. Make sure that as you sand the top flat, its edge is parallel to the upper edge of the inlays.

**10** While the ivory tusk is baking, make two lapis discs. Make one the same size as the top of the ivory tusk and one slightly larger. Assemble them from clumps of lapis mixture: the smaller from a pile about the size of a filbert nut, the larger the size of a pecan. Pinch the edges slightly to taper them. This intentionally delicate edge on an otherwise uniformly thick piece refines the disc.

**11** Pierce a hole in each disc. Poke the needle through from both sides to ensure an even contour on the edges of the hole. This is especially important in a composition material like lapis that may fragment easily.

**12** Bake the pair of discs in a preheated oven for 20 minutes. Remove and let cool.

**13** Finish the lapis discs. The disc on the left below isn't finished. The larger disc on the right has been properly sanded and polished. The metallic leaf has been sanded off the finished lapis's surface, yet the leaf inside the disc is still visible, adding a glimmer.

**14** Make a long eye pin from 12- or 14-gauge wire. This wire must be long enough to go through the bead, the two discs, and penetrate at least 1/2" into the tusk.

**15** Drill a hole the size of the wire you used for the eye pin. If none of your drill bits are the right size, use a drill bit the same size or slightly smaller than the wire. The wire should fit snugly in the hole.

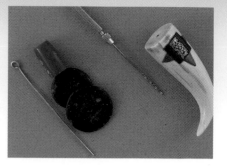

**16** Select a coral bead. If you don't have a premade bead, refer to page 86 for instructions to make a coral bead. Choose a bead with proportions that combine well with the tusk and discs. Have the finished lapis discs ready.

**17** Put the bead and discs on the wire. Before gluing, assemble all the elements to check that they fit together and that you like the look of the piece. Change what's necessary to please you. Set the eye pin in the tusk so its eye is perpendicular to the face of the tusk. Ensure this by holding up the tusk toward you, with the eye pin resting in it but not glued. Turn the eye pin so you don't see the opening of the eye pin, just the edge of the wire loop. This way, when you hang the tusk on a cord, it will face you. See the photo.

**18** Put a couple drops of Zap-a-Gap on the tip of the wire and one drop right into the hole itself. Slide the wire into the hole. Hold the wire securely until the glue sets (about 20 seconds).

**19** Hang the pendant on the black rubber cord. Finish as you prefer, or knot at the back. Very nice!

# jade ginko leaf necklace

for this intermedate
project, you will need:

Fimo Classic
　　1 ounce Art Translucent (#00)
　　pea-size piece of green (#5)
　　half pea-size of purple (#6)
1/2 ounce of the lightest green
　　mix from the jade bowl project
　　(page 82)
acrylic paint: off-white or parch-
　　ment
36" length of Beadalon, Softflex,
　　or other beading cord
2 crimp beads
clasp
string of pearls or other beads

The materials to be used for making
an imitative jade ginko leaf necklace:
clays, jewelry findings, and a length
of inexpensive pearls, which are a
pretty accent to the smooth green
jade.

**Note:** *Detailed information on
basic polymer clay techniques can
be found in Chapter 4, Foundation
Processes.*

## instructions

*1* Mix the green and purple
pea-sized polymer pieces
into the translucent clay. Preheat
the oven, and when it is at temperature, bake a test-piece of this
mix to make sure you like the
color.

*2* Have handy the palest
green from the jade bowl
project, or another jade color
whose relationship with this
green pleases you.

*3* Make an irregularly shaped
pad of the dark green, about
1/4" thick, and two smaller irregular pads of the light green.

*4* Feather the light green
onto the dark green, and
smooth the surface of the pad by
rolling it flat. Allow the pad to
thin to about 3/16".

*5* Cut out the ginko leaf templates for this project (see
page 141), or use designs of your
own to create patterns for the jade
shapes. Arrange them on the feathered polymer pad to take advantage
of attractive shaded areas on the
clay. Use an X-acto knife to cut the
leaves out of the jade polymer.

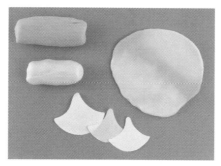

*6* Remove the paper patterns.
Lay each leaf on a small
sheet of paper, which you'll use to
bake the leaf on. A few more steps
convert the cookie cutter look of
this leaf section into a unique
jewelry element.

*7* Pinch the top of the cutout
shape into a more slender
extension of the leaf. As you pinch
it, push the clay closer to the leaf
so that the extension becomes
taller than the surface of the leaf.
Pierce a hole through this extension with the needle tool.
Remember to go in from each end
to create smooth edges to the hole.

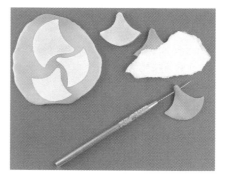

*8* Tear all the sharp edges off a
small scrap of clean white
paper. Lay the paper over the
lower edge of the leaf shape.
Gently press straight down, along
the lower edge of the leaf, to thin
the leaf out at its edge. I use my
index finger for this; it is a gentle
rubbing motion, with a little pressure. Do not emboss the edge of
the paper in the upper section of
the leaf. When finished, a side
view of the leaf should show a
slight taper from the top, where
the pierced extension is a bit
higher, to the lower edge, where
you've just gently pressed the clay
thinner. This process may change
the colors in the feathering at the
lower edge, and you may want to
clean this edge a bit, but leave it
thinner.

*9* Before you bake the leaves,
check for fingerprints on
the clay. Use the same scrap of
paper to burnish out any prints, so
less sanding is required later.
These will be buffed to a high polish, and fingerprints will be quite

obvious. Avoid them now, when it's easy to get rid of them.

**10** From a small scrap of the feathered clay pad, make a short tubular bead, about 3/16" wide or narrower, and about 1" long. Pierce a moderately large hole in it, so that two thicknesses of the stringing cord will easily slide through the hole. Bake this bead and the leaves in a preheated oven for 20 minutes. Remove and let cool.

**11** Cut those ginko-distinguishing notches out of the lower edges of the baked leaves. Wait until now to cut them so you can see how the feathering pebbled after baking, and how the color patterns developed. If there are any attractive areas you want to retain on the leaf, cut the notches somewhere else. Use an X-acto and cut straight down.

**12** Under water, sand the surfaces of each leaf with 400- and 600-grit wet-or-dry sandpaper. Although the backs won't be visible, you will feel them against your skin when you're wearing the necklace, so smooth them off rather than leaving the texture of the baked polymer. Sand over any sharp edges on the clay. Sand off any fingerprints that remain.

**13** The carving pattern for the veins of the leaves is very simple. As shown, carve a shallow crescent into the leaf below the raised extension. The veins will radiate down and out from this curve. A real ginko leaf has many fine veins; however when I carved in that whole waterfall of lines I was not as happy with that effect as with this pattern of just a few lines. Experiment for yourself. When carving the veins, avoid the notch. The veins detour around either side of the notch in a real leaf.

**14** Rub off-white or parchment color acrylic paint in the incised lines, then lighten it somewhat by scrubbing at it with an old, clean toothbrush. This slightly thins the layer of paint without adding water. Play around with this effect. This is a useful way to develop some color in the carved lines without laying a thick opaque mass of acrylic paint into the groove of the line.

**15** Wipe the excess paint off the surface with a slightly damp paper towel. Put the leaves back in the oven for five minutes to set the paint. Remove and let cool.

**16** Sand one last time with 1000-grit sandpaper to establish a very smooth surface for polishing, and to remove any traces of paint from the surface of the leaves. Buff the leaves to a high shine.

**17** String the leaves, adding three pearls between each leaf. This will allow the leaves to overlap in an authentic fashion, adding a nice bit of motion to the necklace when worn. Add enough pearls to create a length you like. I used about 20" of pearls. The necklace is a bit longer because of the clasp and beads.

**18** Retrieve that short narrow tube of jade you made earlier. Sand and polish it. Cut it in two 1/4" sections, finding the areas you like along that inch of jade. Save the rest for another project.

**19** Slip one of the jade tubes onto the string. Slide on the crimp bead. Run the string through the clasp loop or jump ring, and back down through the crimp bead and also through the jade tube. Pull taut, leaving 1/8" or less between the loop and the crimp bead. Flatten the crimp bead on the two sections of the string. Trim the string from below the jade tube. Repeat on the other side of the necklace.

*Note: The reason for the tube is that the drilled holes in pearls are very small, and only one thickness of string will go through them. The jade tube adds a bit of give for you to pull the cord taut, and a place for the end of the string to hide, so it is not sticking out next to the last pearl.*

**20** Now that's lovely! Good job.

# inlaid silver frame

## instructions

*1* Condition the white clay and set it aside.

*2* Find or create a thick 4" by 5" baked pad of polymer clay to make a mold. As with all molds, use well-conditioned and well-baked clay, free of any surface textures. The pad should be 1/4" thick or more.

*3* Carve a crisply defined pattern into the surface of this pad. Use the template on page 140 or create your own. (To transfer the pattern to an unbaked clay pad, burnish a photocopy of it face down on the clay and bake. If transferring after baking, trace the lines in ballpoint pen, press the paper pen-side-down against the pad, and firmly burnish the back of the paper.) Use tools that will make sharp edges and precise shapes: contours associated with metal objects. I used a v-shaped fine linoleum carving blade and a small drill bit to drill straight down, making the small round holes.

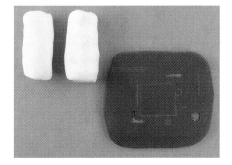

*4* Roll the white polymer to about 1/8" thick. You may use the #1 setting on a pasta machine. Cut a rectangle about 4" by 5" and lay it on a sheet of paper. Roll over it gently to adhere the clay to the paper.

*5* Put on a dust mask and mix about 1/4 teaspoon each of the silver powders together. Coat the surface of the white rectangle. The silver powder will act as the mold release. (You do remember the mold release, right?)

*6* Set the carved plate, carved face down, on the silvered polymer. Roll firmly once over the mold with a glass or press down firmly with your hand, embossing the pattern precisely into the unbaked polymer. Lift the mold and look at the surface. If you do not like it, reuse this clay and repeat these steps until you are satisfied with the surface. Make it just as you want it. To avoid distortion while the clay is so thin, don't cut out the central window until after the frame has been baked.

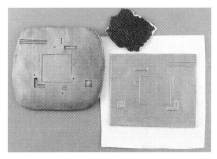

*7* Use a very coarse sandpaper to emboss a scattering of faint pits and eccentricities on the clay. These will mimic natural surface irregularities in the metal.

*8* Trim any wobbly edges of the frame front back to 3-1/2" by 4". Use the underlying paper to transfer the frame to the oven. Bake, remove, and cool. Peel the baked frame off the paper.

*9* Use the template on page 140 to cut out the central window. Make sure the edges of

---

### for this intermediate project, you will need:

Fimo
   4 ounces white (#0)
prebaked inlays of amber, turquoise, lapis, coral
pad of clay to carve mold, at least 3-1/2" by 4", or pre-existing mold for frame surface
powders: Fimo silver metallic powder, PearlEx pigments silver powder
acrylic paint: two brands of silver, burnt umber, and black
Fimo lacquer (optional)

The materials needed to make this picture frame: white polymer clay, prebaked inlays in amber, coral, lapis, and turquoise, a thick baked pad about 4" by 5" to carve into a mold for the frame's surface pattern (or a mold you have already), silver and dark paints and powders, and a small photo.

**Note:** *Detailed information on basic polymer clay techniques can be found in Chapter 4, Foundation Processes.*

the window are crisp before you start to paint the frame.

**10** Mix a dark metallic paint by combining the burnt umber, black, and silver acrylic paints. Look at a true silver object to assess the strong contrast between dark areas and light areas of the metal. This layer of paint will look most realistic if it is quite dark. Rub the dark metallic paint mixture on the surface. Be sure to get it into all the deeper areas on the surface. If necessary, use a stiff brush to poke paint into the pitted areas. Shade the paint over the surface so that open and smooth areas are not as dark. Let dry thoroughly.

**11** To heighten the reflective metallic effect, mix a light bright silver paint by combining the silver acrylic paints with a small amount of silver metallic powder made by combining the Fimo and PearlEx powders.

**12** Lightly brush this bright silver across the highlights of the frame's details. Touch up the tops of the raised lines, dab the paint evenly in unpatterned open areas, and brush it over the crisp edging around the window.

**13** Pause and examine what you have. How does it look? I find that despite my efforts to develop an imitative metals technique that only requires two steps (dark paint, then light), most good-looking imitative metallics usually have extra layers of fussing. Evaluate the frame. If it looks rich and lustrous enough for you, that's great. Skip to the next step. If you want to fiddle and adjust, go ahead. Work back into the surface, maybe add some more dark paint here and there, or more highlighting on the silver edges, or touch up that one area.

Do it now. Just avoid building up a thick, pasty layer of paint, which looks very artificial. Metallic effects must be thinly applied so that crisp details do not lose their precision.

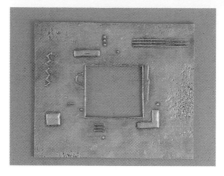

**14** When the paint is acceptable, put the frame back in the oven for 10 minutes to set the paint. Remove and let cool.

**15** Roll the remainder of the white clay out quite thin with a glass or the pasta machine, creating a sheet about 1/16" thick. Roll the clay on a sheet of paper, adhering it to the paper to stabilize and transport the thin frame element. Cut a 3-1/2" by 4" rectangle for the back of the frame.

**16** Roll what's left of the white clay equally thin on another sheet of paper. Cut out an inner layer for the frame. Use the interior layer template on page 140 or your own design. Create a u-shaped element whose opening is about 1/8" larger than the window itself. (Refer to the silver spirals frame on page 104 for assistance.)

**17** Bake these two elements on the paper, remove from the oven, peel off the paper, and let cool. Glue the interior layer onto the frame back, ensuring that the glue seals the margin around the window completely, to avoid trapping the photo.

**18** Mix all the remaining white clay together into a conditioned ball. Create a thick wedge shape. This wedge stand will support the back of the frame. Angle the wedge so the frame will lean back slightly when resting on it.

**19** Bake in a preheated oven for 20 minutes. Remove and let cool. Check the elements for fit and stability of form. Sand away any bumps that keep the back from standing up. Set aside until you can assemble all elements together.

**20** Gather the prebaked inlays you have chosen to add. The template on page 141 shows where the inlays go. If you are using your own pattern, select where you'd like to add color to the frame.

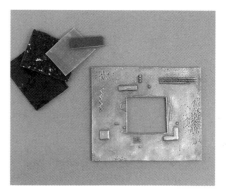

*21* Cut out the shapes of inlays to be added to the frame. The inlays will stick up above the surface of the silver frame. Use a tissue blade to shave them thinner if yours are higher than you'd like. When working with imitative metals, I add inlays on the surface of the frame after baking, rather than pressing them before baking as with other imitative techniques. The silver painting used on the surface of the "metal" cannot be smeared over the inlays and sanded off, as can the antiquing paints used in the other techniques.

*22* Use Zap-a-Gap to glue the inlays on the frame. Be careful to glue the entire area of each inlay. Press each one down securely and hold it until the glue is dry.

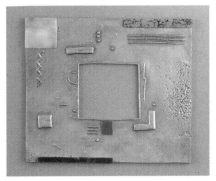

*23* Glue the frame front to the frame back assemblage. Glue the wedge stand to the frame back. Use silver paints to touch up the back, sides, and wedge stamp of this frame. Refer to the silver spirals frame on page 104 if necessary.

*24* Use the size guide of the interior frame element and cut a photo for the frame. Insert the photograph. Fini! Stand it in a prominent spot.

# *agate and gold earrings*

# instructions

*1* Lay the agate slab flat. Cut a rectangular section from the side of the slab about 1/2" wide. Set the rest of the slab aside.

*2* Cut the section in half diagonally, creating two triangles, one with a light base and one with a dark base. Notice that like all right angle triangles, each of these has two perpendicular sides and one diagonal side.

*3* Select one triangle to be worked first and set the other aside.

*4* Stand the triangle up on its diagonal. It is important that the triangle of clay be resting on the diagonal side, not the long perpendicular side. The layers of clay should be angled to the table. If they are perpendicular to the table, please flip the triangle over so that it looks like the photo.

*5* Slice the triangle in half from above, bisecting it into two identical triangles, just like the larger one except half the thickness.

*6* Open the triangles and let them fall to either side of the cut just made. Lay them flat on the table. They will mirror each other as shown. Join the two halves together along the center edge. This center edge was the long perpendicular base of the original triangle. The lines of the layered clay should angle down, like the veins of a leaf.

*7* Press this joint together securely. Pick the leaf up and use your fingers to wiggle the joint until it feels secure. If the layers are coming apart and you are comfortable working with TLS, you may put a very thin line of it along this joint to secure it.

*8* Use a tissue blade to round the upper edge of the leaf shape. (You will be able to adjust this shape by sanding after bak-

## for this intermedate project, you will need:

agate slab, 1/4" to 1/2" thick by 1" square (see page 98 for agate making instructions)

1/2 ounce Fimo golden yellow, or amber mix (see page 90 for amber making instructions)

mold for earring top, or baked pad of clay to carve mold

powders: Fimo gold metallic powder, PearlEx pigments gold powder

acrylic paint: bronze, iridescent gold, iridescent bright gold

6" length of 18-gauge gold-colored wire

earring backs

Agate and gold earrings first require an angled slab of agate—one in which the layers are at an angle to the surface of the slab, rather than perpendicular. Use the basic agate from page 98 or make another block, perhaps trying different colors.

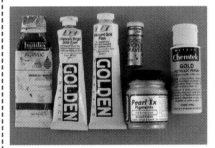

The paints and powders required to mimic gold: Metallic finishes benefit from a rich combination of powders and paints. Even if your assortment varies from mine, having an assortment rather than one paint and one powder is what is most important.

**Note:** *Detailed information on basic polymer clay techniques can be found in Chapter 4, Foundation Processes.*

ing, so don't worry about it being perfect at this point.)

**9** Retrieve the set aside triangle from step 3 and repeat these steps (slice it in half, join, trim to round at the top). The second earring will be black on top and light at the bottom, the opposite of the first.

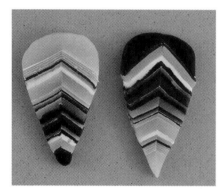

**10** In a preheated oven, bake both agate pieces for 20 minutes. Turn the oven off and let the pieces cool in the oven.

**11** After the leaf pieces have cooled, sand them by hand or with a belt sander. Refine the shapes and sand off all the smeared surface clay, revealing the crisp layering of the imitative agate.

**12** Carve a small round patterned mold to use for the gold earring tops. You may design your own pattern or use the one on page 141. First bake a smooth, flat pad of light-colored polymer. Transfer or draw the template on its surface, then use a fine v-shaped carving blade to carve the pattern. Use a fine drill bit to gently hand drill holes in the baked clay. Remember that the earring tops will be the size of the mold you create, so think about the size of your earlobes and what will work there.

**13** Take a positive from this mold to check the appearance of the pattern. Notice the fine precise raised lines arising from the v-shaped blade and the delicate round knobs from the holes drilled in the polymer. Also check the size of the earring tops to make sure they will look right on your ears. (Another option, not shown, is to use an all-over pattern, emboss it on the polymer, and isolate a section that is the appropriate size.)

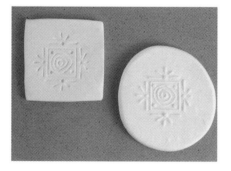

**14** Use amber mix or other golden yellow polymer to make two small balls of clay. Roll these until they have no folds or seams. Flatten them slightly into pads.

**15** Thoroughly mix 1/8 teaspoon each of the gold powders together. Coat the clay pads with this mix, front and back, to serve as a mold release

and also enhance the metallic effect.

**16** Press each pad of powdered clay onto the mold. Either roll over each once with a glass to strongly emboss the pattern, or press with your fingers, taking care not to shift the clay and blur the pattern. Check the embossing. If you do not like it, mix the polymer back into a ball, repowder, and repeat. There's no reason to accept something you don't like.

**17** Cut a circle from each of the embossed pads. Use circle cutters if you have them, or cut the circles freehand.

**18** In a preheated oven, bake the circular earring tops for 30 minutes. Remove and let cool.

**19** Check the thickness of the baked gold circles. These discs must be thick enough to accommodate an eye pin for hanging the agate leaves. If they are too thin, add clay to the back and rebake.

**20** Mix the gold paints together to a light gold color, and lightly highlight the upper edges of the pattern. Gently dab the light gold on the open areas of the pattern. Adjust the painting until you are satisfied. Everyone's touch with the paints is different. One set of instructions will not address all individual styles in the application of paint. Much of making successful imitative metallics comes from working with the surface until your unique combination of paints, your way of applying paint, your eye for color and patina, all come together.

**21** Make four eye pins from the 18-gauge gold-colored wire. Two will go in the discs, two in the leaves.

**22** Drill holes in the discs and the leaves, for the eye pins. When drilling the holes in the leaves, use a bit as close to the gauge of the wire as possible. The agate leaves are thin, and the eye pin will be set along the joint of the polymer layers in the agate. If the wire is thicker than the hole, it will push the joint open and may separate the layers a bit, which is not good.

**23** Glue the eye pins in each section of each earring. Let the glue dry. The upper and lower eye pins must be set perpendicular to each other, so they hang straight. I routinely set eye pins in upper earring elements parallel to the face of the tops. Then I set eye pins in lower earring elements perpendicular to the face of the dangling piece. Here, the eye pins in the gold discs face out and the ones in the leaves are perpendicular. This also lowers the visible profile of the eye pins.

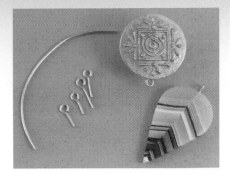

**24** Glue the earring backs to the back of the gold discs. Let the glue dry.

**25** Attach the eye pins of the earring elements, joining the gold discs and agate leaves. Put them on and admire what a beautiful pair of earrings you made!

# gallery

Photo by the artist.

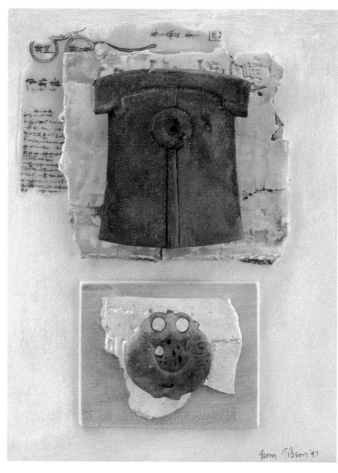

Photo by Robert Diamanti.

ABOVE: Nan Roche, *Pendant,* 2002. Roche is the author of *The New Clay,* and an accomplished artist herself. Here she mimics the feel of Japanese lacquer, synthesizing aspects of the imitative and mokume gane techniques to create a rich, time-worn effect distinctively her own. Very thin layers of carefully chosen colors were embossed, then sanded away, allowing each color to shadow over another.

TOP RIGHT: Gwen Gibson, *Wall Piece,* 1997. Gibson seamlessly merges surface and form in this exotic assemblage. Much of her personal style is based on the random gesture. The clay's edge happens to rip like this, and she leaves it; or the paint happens to smear like that, and she leaves it. She grounds this dance of serendipity in a deep knowledge of paints and patinas. Knowing when to maintain and when to release control is a definition of mastery.

RIGHT: Deborah Anderson, *Box,* 2001. Anderson's re-creations of old hand-tooled leatherwork integrate many of polymer's best qualities. Her understanding of color, opacity, surface, and patina displayed in this box wonderfully illustrate her use of imitative techniques to pursue her own direction in the medium. Personal touches take the traditions of the original material to a new level, like adding the dimensional dragonflies to the exterior of this box.

Photo by Liv Ames.

Photo by the artist.

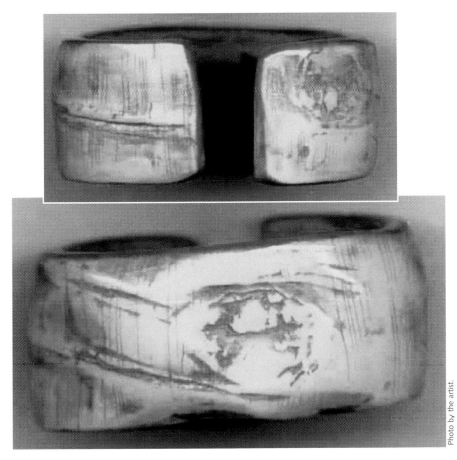

Photo by the artist.

Top left: Jean Cohen, *Brooch,* 1999. Cohen's sense of pattern and design reads clearly in this brooch. Combining deeply textured ivory and jade imitatives with a striking gold and black mokume gane section, the overall effect is strong and rich. By running the jade calligraphy upside down, its abstract shapes relate more easily to the triangles on the ivory areas.

Above: Nan Roche, *Pendant,* 2002. Roche's sophisticated blend of exterior shape, controlled layering of clay bodies, surface colors and textures, and final patina come together in a beautiful pendant. The matte, dusty copper patina in the embossed calligraphy is an especially nice touch. Notice her elegant finishing of the necklace: minimal black accents on a black rubber cord that encourage our focus on the sumptuous lacquerlike surface.

Left and inset: Paulo Guimaraes, *Bracelet,* 1999. Guimaraes' observation of qualities and his deft confidence with texture and paint hallmark this bracelet. Organic irregularities on its surfaces heighten the natural amber luminosity of color and shading. Attention to all the surfaces, including the interior coloring, lets the observer know the artist is in complete control of the piece, and knows when to allow variation and randomness.

Photo by Robert Diamanti.

ABOVE: Gwen Gibson, *Object*, 2000. Gibson's artistic confidence sings in this elemental form, treated to convey great age and potency. A long-time commitment to her creative life allows this spontaneity in her wonderful pieces.

TOP RIGHT: Liz Tamayo, *Brooch*, 1999. Tamayo's personal style resonates throughout this brooch. After modeling the small face, she set it on an etched-looking pattern reminiscent of faraway stone carvings, using Gwen Gibson's tear-away transfer technique. The beaded edging and the lacy ivory-colored heishi looped in along the bottom invite our visual and tactile interest, and further evoke the South Sea Islands.

RIGHT: Tom Plattenberger, *Box*, 1998. Plattenberger's strong engineering sense shows in the system he developed for re-creating stone. By baking a mixture of baked and unbaked polymer granules and nonpolymer materials between glass, he generates evenly thick, wonderfully mottled slabs of glossy smoothness. This precisely shaped box was constructed from such slabs. An interior sleeve of similar stonelike material fits perfectly, supporting the lid.

Photo by Don Haab.

Photo by the artist.

Photo by Don Haab.

TOP LEFT: Jacqueline Lee, *Floral Inro,* 1999. Lee assembled this piece from a collection of different molded floral elements taken from antique Japanese metalwork. Her initial clay body is a carefully controlled blend of black and bronze clays and metallic powders, and this care extends to the mixture of four different bronzing powders for the rich metallic highlights on the chrysanthemums.

ABOVE: Paulo Guimaraes, *Necklace,* 1999. Guimaraes, a doctor in Brazil, has expanded on the imitative techniques to re-create his area's natural and cultural artifacts. This traditionally strung necklace, shown here in detail, shows his exacting polymer imitations of beetle wings. After making a mold of the inside and outside of several wings, he carefully colored them with iridescent pigments, then drilled and strung them.

LEFT: Jacqueline Lee, *Peony Box,* 2000. Lee replicates the sophisticated presence of Japanese antiquities. Her work reveals her sensitive eye for texture, a real mastery of making and using molds, and exquisite workmanship. The contrast here of peonies' smooth gilded petals over the roughened matte background creates the effect of gold-washed cast iron or bronze.

Photo by the artist.

ABOVE: Cheryl Trottier, *Sculpture,* 2000. Trottier sculpted this small, charming sea otter from an imitative ivory, and added black polymer for nose and eyes. Although diminutive and loosely modeled, its personality comes across clearly, as does the artist's love for her subject.

TOP RIGHT: Dayle Doroshow, *Ancestral Memory,* sculpture, 2001. Doroshow's fascination with mixed media blends with a long-time interest in faces in this haunting sculptural piece. The face is fabricated from polymer and aged, its expression conveying an enigmatic, ancient simplicity. Wrapping patterned clay in subdued colors around a wooden core embodies the figure. Doroshow exhibits her signature style: immediacy of workmanship in the service of artistic integrity.

RIGHT: Christopher Knoppel, *Brooch,* 1999. Knoppel's sense of form and strong design gestures show to good advantage in this elegant, understated brooch. A tear-away transfer etches the line drawing into the ivory-colored polymer. Simple faceted silver beads outline the beveled edges around an attractively asymmetrical contour.

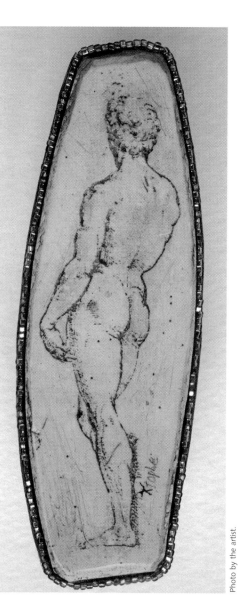

Photo by Don Felton.

Photo by the artist.

Photo by Kojo Kamau.

Photo by the artist.

TOP LEFT: Debora Jackson, *African Shrine*, neckpiece, 2000. Jackson works from her heritage, blending technique with concept and truly personalizing her art. Here, bold line carving enhances the strong shapes of the ivory elements in a powerful neckpiece. By adding the slight asymmetry, she confidently uses the principles of design to support her ideas, taking control as an artist.

ABOVE: Christopher Knoppel, *Necklace*, 1998. Knoppel created this bold, assured ivory and coral necklace. He chose abstract forms for the large molded beads and integrated them with imitative coral and real silver. An unusual composition complements the unique shapes of the beads.

LEFT: Stacia Schwartz, *Brooch*, 2001. Schwartz took a direct, confident approach to this charming ivory rabbit, which was transferred and carved, then antiqued.

Photo by Elise Winter.

Victoria Hughes has been making and selling artwork in polymer clay for more than 30 years. She started her business, first named Art for Life, now the ArtRanch, in 1982. She has been a self-supporting artist all her life. Her development and use of innovative techniques like the imitatives has influenced a generation of polymer clay artists, both through her jewelry and sculpture, seen in galleries nationwide and numerous publications, and her teaching career, which has spanned the United States and Canada. In the mid-1990s, Hughes finished a series of 15 instructional videos detailing the techniques she has developed and refined.

Hughes developed the imitative techniques in 1992. The techniques and the component processes have permeated artists' response to polymer clay, so that sanding, polishing, antiquing, and other elements of these techniques are commonplace. In fact, after the first article about these techniques appeared in *Ornament Magazine* in 1992, Eberhard Faber formulated a line of imitative polymer clays and you can now buy clays called "lapis," "jade," and others. (They are not substitutes for the realism of Hughes' actual techniques.)

Hughes continues to invent new imitative techniques as well as explore new, unrelated possibilities of polymer clay and mixed media. The material continues to evolve, and the edges of its potential are uncharted territory. Hughes is most comfortable investigating the unknown landscape and bringing back information. Her ultimate interest is in creativity itself, and she sees a perfect fit between the responsiveness and versatility of polymer clay and this art material, which supports her understanding and expression of the creative process as an artist and teacher.

The Good Grid

| | | |
|---|---|---|
| | | |
| | | |
| | | |
| | | |
| | | |
| | | |

Make several copies and staple them together for your logbook.
Glue on baked samples and add notes.

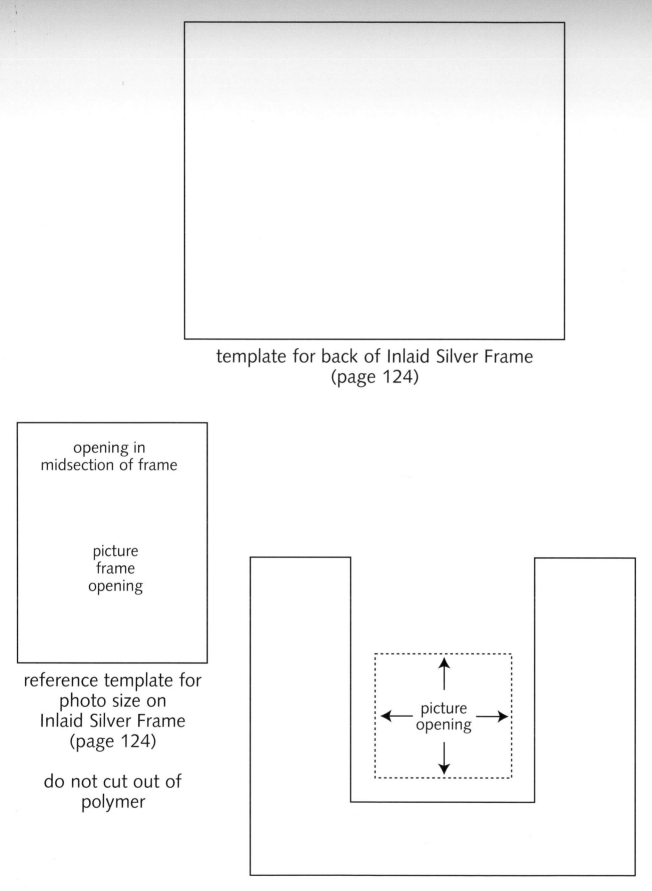

template for back of Inlaid Silver Frame
(page 124)

opening in
midsection of frame

picture
frame
opening

reference template for
photo size on
Inlaid Silver Frame
(page 124)

do not cut out of
polymer

picture
opening

template for midsection of Inlaid Silver Frame
(page 124)

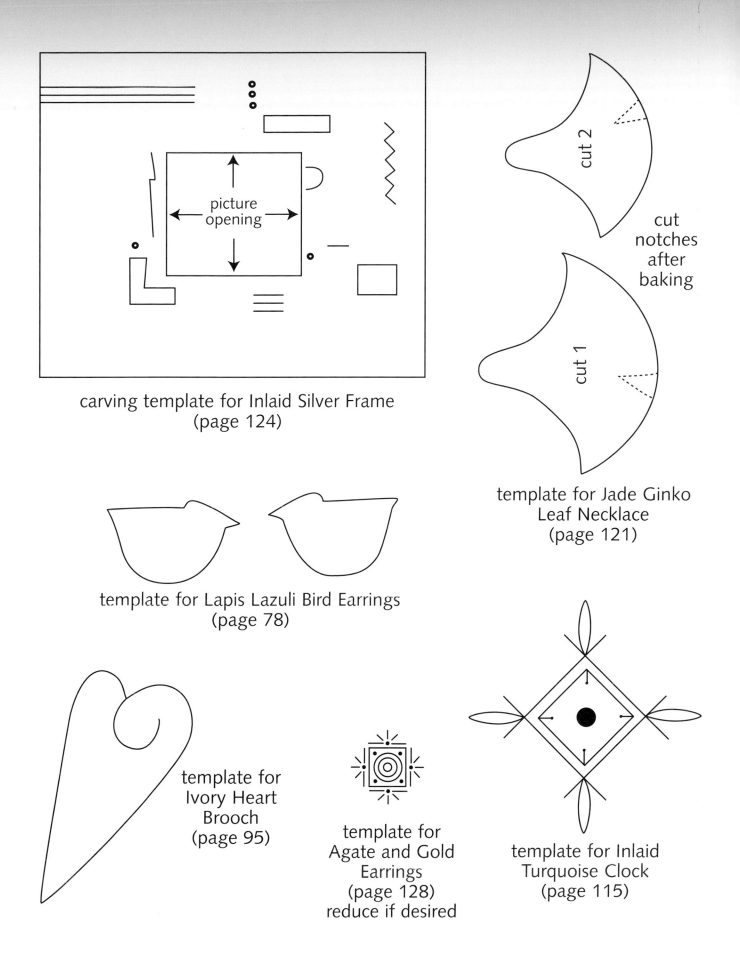

carving template for Inlaid Silver Frame
(page 124)

picture
opening

cut 2

cut 1

cut
notches
after
baking

template for Jade Ginko
Leaf Necklace
(page 121)

template for Lapis Lazuli Bird Earrings
(page 78)

template for
Ivory Heart
Brooch
(page 95)

template for
Agate and Gold
Earrings
(page 128)
reduce if desired

template for Inlaid
Turquoise Clock
(page 115)

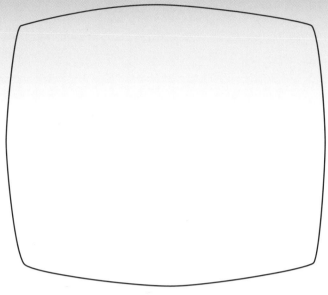

template for Silver Spirals Frame back
(page 104)

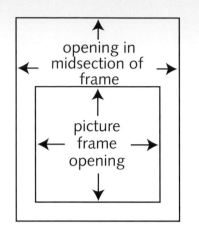

reference template for photo
size on Silver Spirals Frame
back (page 104)

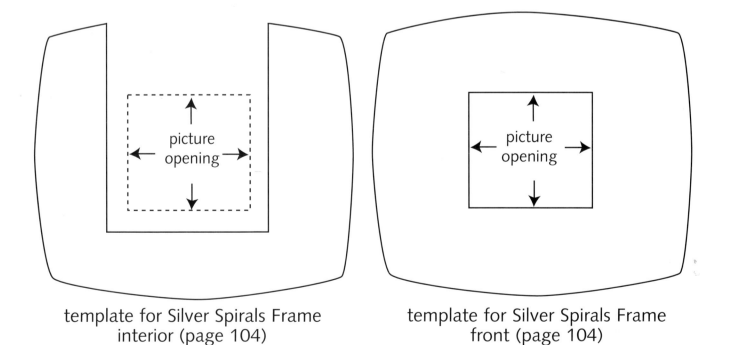

template for Silver Spirals Frame
interior (page 104)

template for Silver Spirals Frame
front (page 104)

# resources

## suppliers and contacts

*Below are just a few of the larger suppliers of polymer clay and related materials. Additional information can be found by perusing the ads in related magazines. The polymer clay community is extremely active online, so if you are too, search and browse for a much wider supply of information, contacts, resources, and events.*

### polymer clay and related materials

**The Clay Factory**
(877) SCULPEY
www.clayfactoryinc.com

**FIMOZONE** (aka Accent Import Export)
(800) 989-2889
www.fimozone.com

**Polymer Clay Express/The ArtWay Studio**
(800) 844-0138
www.polymerclayexpress.com

### jewelry supplies and findings

**Rio Grande**
(800) 545-6566
www.riogrande.com

**Rings and Things**
(800) 366-2156
www.rings-things.com

**Fire Mountain Gems**
(800) 355-2137
www.firemountaingems.com

**Soft Flex Company**
(707) 938-3539
www.softflexcompany.com

## organizations

**National Polymer Clay Guild**
1350 Beverly Road
Suite 115-345
McLean, VA 22101
www.npcg.org
*wide-ranging polymer clay information, good web site and a newsletter*

**Bead Society of Greater Washington**
(301) 277-6830
www.bsgw.org
*Bead societies are often a good resource for classes in polymer and jewelry. This society may be able to guide you to one near you.*

## library

### information about polymer clay

**Mastering the New Clay**
Tory Hughes
Gameplan/ArtRanch
Productions, 1995, 1999, 2002
(510) 549-0993
www.gameplanvideo.com
*18-volume instructional video series*

**Foundations in Polymer Clay Design**
Barbara McGuire
Krause Publications, 1999
(800) 258-0929
www.krause.com

**The New Clay**
Nan Roche
Flower Valley Press, 1991

**Creating with Polymer Clay**
Stephen Ford and Leslie Dierks
Lark Books, 1995

### books for the artist's studio

**Collectible Beads—A Universal Aesthetic**
Robert K. Liu
Ornament Inc., 1995
*beautiful closeup photographs and scholarly text*

**The History of Beads—From 30,000 BC to the Present**
Lois Sherr Dubin
Harry N. Abrams, 1987
*pantheon of beads, their uses and materials*

**Ethnic Jewelry**
John Mack, ed.
Harry N. Abrams, 1988
*cross-cultural approaches to adornment*

**Africa Adorned**
Angela Fisher
Harry N. Abrams, 1984
*the classic, full-page luscious photos of adornments*

**Buttons**
Diana Epstein and Millicent Safro
Harry N. Abrams, 1991
*wide variety of materials and techniques, in miniature*

**Amber—Window to the Past**
David A. Grimaldi
Harry N. Abrams, 1996
*good photos; from Natural History Museum Show*

*Ojime–Magical Jewels of Japan*
Robert O. Kinsey
Harry N. Abrams, 1991
*good resource, many photos of beautiful small objects*

**Treasures of the Dark Ages in Europe**
Ariadne Galleries, 1991
*nice photos of old metal, unusual forms*

**Victorian Jewelry–Unexplored Treasures**
Ginny Dawes and Corrine Davidov
Abbeville Press, 1991
*primarily beautiful agates and jaspers set in silver*

**Crossroads of Continents–Cultures of Siberia and Alaska**
William Fitzhugh and Aron Crowell
Smithsonian Institution Press, 1988
*a wealth of unusual objects and information*

**Gifts of the Nile–Ancient Egyptian Faience**
Florence Dunn Friedman, ed.
Thames and Hudson, 1998
*gorgeous, extensive, beautiful resource*

**Art and Craft in Africa–Everyday Life/Ritual/Court Art**
Laurie Meyer
Terrail, English edition, 1995
*high-quality objects and photos, exquisite art*

**Ancient Iranian Ceramics–from the Arthur M. Sackler Collections**
Trudy S. Kawami
Harry N. Abrams, 1992
*wonderful and inventive forms*

**The Spirited Earth–Dance, Myth and Ritual from South Asia to the South Pacific**
Victoria Ginn
Rizzoli, 1990
*copious, lovely photographs, shows museum pieces in use in life*

**Glorious Inspirations**
Kaffe Fassett
Random House, 1991, rep.
Sterling Publishing
*wonderful variety of surfaces*

Sotheby's auction house in New York publishes catalogs of its various sales. These are nicely photographed and printed, and of good-quality items with descriptions. For instance, one I refer to is *Important Chinese Snuff Bottles–Sale* 6962, March 17, 1997. It includes jade, agates, inner painted glass, and other materials. Their catalogs are around $25 and can be ordered directly from them.

## periodicals

**Ornament Magazine**
(800) 888-8950
ornament@cts.com
*the classic and sumptuous quarterly of ethnic and contemporary adornment*

**The Crafts Report**
(800) 777-7098
www.craftsreport.com
*useful monthly magazine applicable to all aspects of fine craft business*

**Metalsmith**
(630) 579-3272
www.snagmetalsmith.org
*quarterly about contemporary art/fine craft jewelry and the artists*

**Fiberarts**
(828) 253-0467
www.fiberartsmagazine.com
*quarterly about contemporary textiles, functional and decorative, and artists*

## books for the inner artist
*books that inspire and vitalize you for any reason will benefit your creative process*

**Drawing on the Right Side of the Brain**
Betty Edwards, Jeremy Tarcher

**A Life in the Arts–Practical Guidance & Inspiration for Creative & Performing Artists**
Erik Maisel
Tarcher/Putnam, 1992, 1994

**Art and Fear–Observations on the Perils (and Rewards) of Artmaking**
David Boyles and Ted Orland
Capra Press, 1994

**Trust the Process–An Artist's Guide to Letting Go**
Shaun McNiff
Shambala, 1998